ICT for Teaching Assistants

John Galloway

 David Fulton Publishers

David Fulton Publishers Ltd
The Chiswick Centre, 414 Chiswick High Road, London W4 5TF

www.fultonpublishers.co.uk

First published in Great Britain in 2004 by David Fulton Publishers
10 9 8 7 6 5 4 3 2 1

Note: The right of John Galloway to be identified as the author of this work has been asserted by him in accordance with the Copyright, Designs and Patents Act 1988.

David Fulton Publishers is a division of Granada Learning Limited, part of ITV plc.

Copyright © John Galloway 2004

British Library Cataloguing in Publication Data
A catalogue record for this book is available from the British Library.

ISBN 1 84312 203 0

Typeset by Servis Filmsetting Ltd, Manchester
Printed and bound in Spain

Contents

Introduction

There have been two significant changes in British schools in the last few years: one is an increase in the number of computers, the other is an increase in the number of adults helping pupils to learn. Both are having a marked impact on what is happening in classrooms. While computers are powerful tools for learning, they are of little use without people to guide that learning. This book is intended to help you make better use of these tools.

One of the great things about using computers is that there is always something new to be learnt, not just because programs are always being updated, but also because there is so much to know, so many things that programs can do and so many different ways to do them. It is improbable that any individual knows everything about every piece of software in today's classrooms. Computers have a democratising effect on learning, where it becomes a two-way street with everybody, staff and pupils, teaching each other.

This book cannot tell you all you need to know about teaching and learning with computers, and even if it could I would be wary of denying anyone the pleasure of having even the youngest children show them how to do something, even if they have come across it by accident. While this technology can be enormously frustrating, a satisfying aspect is in getting round the barriers, in achieving something when you know the machine will do it but you just cannot work out how. And when you do work it out you achieve results that, in appearance at the very least, can be as good as the professionals'.

With the accelerating growth of human knowledge, the Internet lets us access and share ideas in ways that have never before been possible. Certainly a lot of what we find on the Internet is of dubious value, but we can also find great works of literature, first-hand accounts of events, live images from faraway countries, and we can make contact with people in classrooms and other interesting locations all over the world.

You will find here ideas about the role of computers in education, about how

ICT is taught as a subject then used to support learning in other subjects, and ideas for how to use them with pupils in classrooms.

Recently the Local Government National Training Organisation (LGNTO) has issued *National Occupational Standards for Teaching Assistants*, which sets out your role in the classroom. These have been developed into a National Vocational Qualification (NVQ) across the UK (the SNVQ in Scotland). This book intends to cover the 'Knowledge Base' for this qualification and point out what you need to do for the 'Performance Indicators'. Coverage of NVQ/SNVQ standards can be found in the appendix.

The relevant NVQ unit 3-17 is split into two sections numbered 1 and 2. Each individual element then has its own reference, numbers for 'Performance indicators' and letters for 'Knowledge base'. So the first criterion, 'Confirm the requirements for ICT equipment with the teacher', is referred to as 3-17.1,1, and so on. I have put them in brackets in the text where relevant.

You will also see some words in bold. These are actions on the computer, either a sequence to follow to get something to happen or a button to press such as **Back** or **Print**. Key terms appear within quotes.

This book is intended to be informative and instructive, helping you to become even more effective in the changing classrooms of the twenty-first century.

John Galloway
May 2004

PART 1

ICT and learning

CHAPTER 1

How we learn and how computers help us

Our job is to help children to learn. This means that all the time we are thinking about what our pupils need to learn and how that can best be achieved. Some of them will bury themselves in books for long periods, while others find it hard just to sit still, so we have to tailor what we do to help them.

The introduction of computers into classrooms has brought about new tools for doing this. Quite often working on a computer engages most (but not all) learners for longer periods than they would be otherwise and enables them to become more creative while working with the powerful tools on offer. Computers also give quick and easy access to all sorts of knowledge. We no longer need to hold facts for quick recall, we need to know how to find them. Learning about things is shifting towards learning about learning.

How human beings learn is the subject of constant research and debate. Understanding of how the brain works is developing all the time, giving rise to new theories about how we gain, store and retrieve knowledge.

We know that learning involves more than simply sitting quietly while someone at the front talks to us. And that people do not absorb everything they read or write down. In fact, people generally learn about:

10 per cent of what they read

20 per cent of what they hear

30 per cent of what they see

50 per cent of what they both hear and see

70 per cent of what they say

90 per cent of what they simultaneously say and do

(Ekwall and Shanker 1988)

So to teach our pupils effectively we need to think about how we can use a variety of different ways to get our message across. Simply reading is the least effective way of learning. Computers are very powerful tools for changing how we work.

Theories of learning

Staff in schools adopt very practical approaches in reaching their charges, often being not too concerned with the theory as long as it works. Very few teachers consciously work with one particular theory or another. It is worth spending some time thinking about them though, particularly when it comes to information and communication technology (ICT), as software is often written from a particular perspective and may or may not suit what we are teaching. The terms 'IT' (information technology) and 'ICT' are often used interchangeably. In schools IT generally refers to the equipment and ICT to what we do with it.

There are two main theories about how we learn: Behaviourism and Constructivism. Both are in evidence in our classrooms today. Most teachers will, probably without knowing it, use different strategies that fall into both categories.

In Behaviourist theory, knowledge is seen as a change in behaviour, with our internal processes, such as thinking and remembering, being types of behaviour. Learning then becomes a process of imparting a body of knowledge to our pupils through a process of changing what they do.

We can see this in primary schools today in the use of rote learning. Times tables are often learnt by saying them out loud in unison. Children can learn that 'seven eights are 56' even if they do not understand how the sum comes about. Very young children repeat the alphabet even when they do not know which letter matches which sound, or even that they are different sounds. Eventually changing how they behave will change their understanding.

The second theory, Constructivism, is based on the idea that we all have our own, unique understanding of the world which we build as we learn new things. As we gain new knowledge, so we fit it into place and move what we already know around so as to accommodate this, like a giant jigsaw where we move the pieces around to fit each time we find a new bit. This is the basis of discovery learning, where pupils are offered experiences from which they then extract their own learning. We could think of project work as Constructivist, where pupils follow their own course in learning.

Both theories have their supporters and their critics. Behaviourism is thought to be too restrictive, while Constructivism could mean pupils miss out on learning key knowledge. So what we tend to do in schools is use a bit of both. Although children might chant times tables, they will also be colouring in number squares to spot the patterns the tables make. Sometimes we teach children the outcome and let the underpinning concepts follow, and sometimes we let them discover the concepts and point out particular outcomes later. In maths we might let pupils try out different ways of doing sums before showing them the standard notation.

Computers themselves can be geared to either way of learning. They are tools that we adapt to our particular methods. Software can be seen as being developed from either perspective. 'Speaking Starspell', for instance, is Behaviourist. It is based on the 'Look, Cover, Write, Check' method of learning spelling. The learner is shown a word, it is taken off screen, they then type it in. If correct they get a reward – 'Well done' – if not they get to try again. While this can be an effective way of working, on its own it can lead to a rather boring educational diet.

Constructivist approaches can be seen in 'Logo' style programs such as '2Go' from 2Simple and 'Softease Turtle' from Softease. Here pupils can build shapes from clicking on arrows through to complex programming. They start from scratch and build their own models. Teachers will provide the challenges, but pupils will learn through trying things out rather than being directly told.

Learning styles

We have five senses and, unless one or more is severely impaired, we learn through all of them. In schools we generally work with sound and vision, reinforced with some tactile experiences, generally ignoring taste and smell. However, you will probably have experienced the situation where a certain smell reminds you of a past event. We can harness all the senses in our work, although not always with a computer. (Sadly the only computer-generated smell is usually a troubling one that irritates the nostrils and is to do with dust on the tube, or wires fusing inside the case. If you experience this you may well remember it, particularly if it is accompanied by wisps of smoke.)

There has been a lot of interest in recent years about learning styles. The Key Stage 3 strategy has several booklets with titles such as *Learning Styles and Writing in English* (DfES 2002).

As well as visual learning (seeing), there is auditory learning (hearing) and kinaesthetic learning (moving or feeling). We can see these in action in acquiring literacy skills when pupils are learning letter shapes and sounds and each has an action linked to it. For example, the 'ess' sound of the letter 'S' is associated with the fingers slithering along the forearm like a snake.

The diagram also refers to 'interpersonal' and 'intrapersonal' learning. The first of these is simply working with others in ways such as discussing and collaborating. The latter is about internal processes, reflecting and thinking about what something means to the individual.

Computers can be a multi-sensory medium, combining sound and visuals in lively and stimulating ways which encourage learning. They are also great for

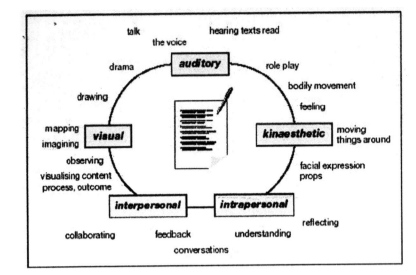

Figure 1.1 *Learning styles*

group work. This is easy in classrooms with interactive whiteboards where everybody can see what is presented and join in the discussion. However, even a standard monitor can be shared by small groups and pairs.

Collaboration becomes possible not only when sitting next to each other but also, through the use of email and chat, from virtually anywhere in the world. Pupils in different schools, in different continents even, can work together. One group can write the first paragraph of a story for the next to continue; photos, drawings and diagrams can be shared and commented on; data about local environments can be exchanged. A useful project is to compare the prices of common items, such as a Big Mac or a Mars Bar. Not only does this demonstrate how costs vary, but it is also a maths exercise in converting currencies and a sociological one on globalisation.

As for personal reflection, these machines allow us the opportunity to change and develop our thoughts quite easily. Given the opportunity to edit, we seldom stick with what we first write. We do not quite get it right, our ideas develop, we think or feel differently. On a screen we can see it all there and alter it until we get what we want.

Some software, such as 'Inspiration', is designed to help us think.

While it looks like a brainstorm, it will organise thoughts into structured levels for things such as essay writing or presentations. This can be used for whole-class work or for individuals to sort out their own ideas.

Multiple intelligences

In 1983 Howard Gardner suggested that human beings have seven different intelligences, although he has recently revised this to eight. He believes that all of them

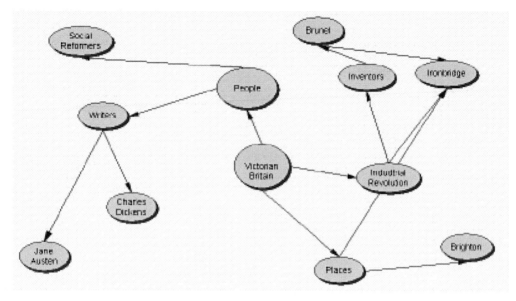

Figure 1.2 *A brainstorm with Inspiration*

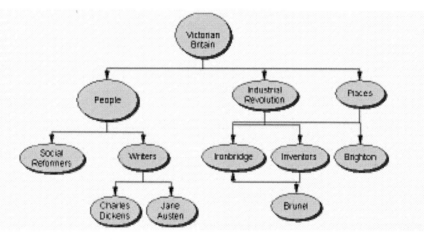

Figure 1.3 *The brainstorm reordered*

are equally important but that in schools we generally only value verbal and computational abilities, that is the way we use language and work things out. These tend to be what we measure through testing and assessment, and what we reward through certification.

The eight intelligences Gardner suggests are:

- logical-mathematical – such as detecting patterns and reasoning things out;
- linguistic – using language both orally and in writing, such as discussions or writing poems;
- spatial – able to manipulate images mentally;
- musical – can recognise elements of music and make up tunes;

- bodily-kinaesthetic – able to co-ordinate one's own movements;

- interpersonal – having an empathy for others, how they think and feel;

- intrapersonal – being aware of our own thoughts and feelings;

- naturalist – aware of one's environment.

This is not to say that we can only learn in particular ways, simply that each of us has different strengths and we should look to exploit all of them in our teaching and learning. All of us have these abilities to some degree, but we all use some more successfully than others.

Computers allow us to work with all these different aspects of our pupils' intelligences. We can compose tunes, write, express our thoughts in many different ways, do endless sums and experiment with numbers.

Knowing about pupils' multiple intelligences can help us to teach to their strengths. Some websites have self-assessment tools to help us to understand our own intelligences. At www.ooshl.org there is a quiz which will show pupils their profile. While we may not be able to teach to their strengths all the time, it will help them to take some control of their own learning and to complete tasks in ways that they find easiest. This is not to say that if they do not have strong logical-mathematical skills they can stop doing sums. Just that they, and you, can look for ways of reinforcing learning through their strengths.

You probably do this anyway, recognising that some prefer to work in certain ways. For instance, instead of writing up a science experiment, you might ask a student to create a flow chart of the procedures, a more spatially inclined way of recording. Or perhaps ask a more musical individual to create a rap to remember a spelling or times table.

Whatever the task, talking helps to reinforce learning. Ask your pupils to describe what they are doing, to talk through the steps of a task. Get them to explain how they have worked something out or how they know a particular answer. This is as valuable in ICT as in any other subject.

One of the great things about working with computers is that we are constantly learning from each other. No matter how confident and experienced we are, other people may have a different way of doing something, a quicker short cut, a more useful tool. It is almost impossible to know every aspect of every program so quite often opportunities are presented to allow the pupils to take the lead and show us what to do.

Summary

We have five senses, eight intelligences, two sides to the brain, two contradictory theories of learning and about a dozen subjects to deliver. While it may seem difficult to juggle it all, ICT offers many possibilities. In some senses it can become an extension to our own brains, a place where we can find knowledge and be creative in hitherto impossible ways. In constructing our own understanding we can bring these machines to bear in a way no other tool allows.

All of us learn differently. Some of our pupils, those with special educational needs (SEN), have very particular learning needs. However, the more we can teach to the broad panorama of learning, the less we will have to make specific, special accommodations for pupils. The need will not have gone away, but more pupils will be engaged with learning for more of the time. Computers are powerful tools for making this possible.

CHAPTER 2

Including all learners

There has been a shift in recent years from a narrow focus on SEN to a broader one on inclusion. This means meeting the individual learning needs not just of those with special needs, but of all pupils. This chapter will consider some of the different groups the term has come to cover, including those who are learning English as an additional language (EAL), and the gifted and talented.

Special educational needs

Computers can offer access to the curriculum for pupils with SEN in ways that other tools for learning cannot. There are two main ways to do this. We can either change how the computer works or we can add to it in some way. This is true for both hardware and software.

Changing what you already have

Whether you are using a Windows (PC) or Apple Macintosh machine, you will find that built into the computer's operating system are ways to change how it looks, works and responds to the user.

In Windows there are a number of ways of adapting the machine to the needs of the individual. You will find these in the **Accessories** section of the **Start** menu. In Windows XP follow **Start>All Programs>Accessories>Accessibility**. The **Accessibility Wizard** helps users to make changes to adapt the computer when they tick one or more of the following options:

I am blind or have difficulty seeing things on the screen.

I am deaf or have difficulty hearing sounds from the computer.

I have difficulty using the keyboard or mouse.

I want to set administrative options.

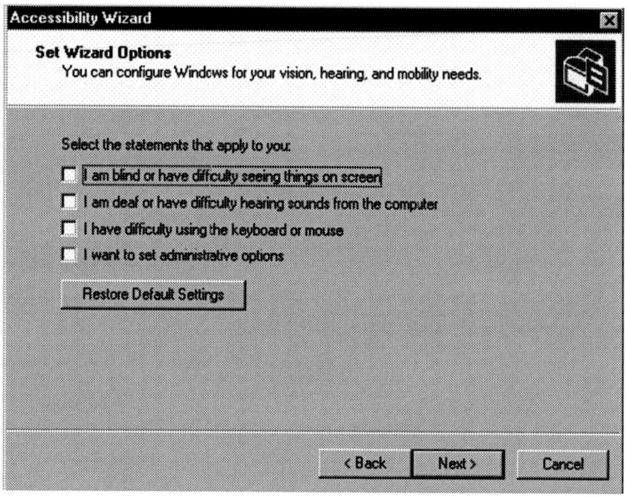

Figure 2.1 *The Accessibility Wizard statements*

The wizard then offers choices for different screen elements such as contrast, size of icons, whether the computer should ignore extra key presses and so on. All these are also available in the **Control Panels** which we shall get to shortly.

Also in the **Accessibility** folder in Windows XP is the **Magnifier** which will enlarge sections of the screen to make it easier to see; **Narrator** which will read any text on the screen and will read descriptions of images on web pages when they are provided; **On-Screen Keyboard** which allows users to use a mouse to select keys instead of their fingers; and **Utility Manager** which will let users decide when to turn the other options on. Some versions of Windows XP also have speech recognition software built in to them which means that users can dictate directly on to their computer.

There are also other ways of altering the computer through the **Control Panel.** The **Accessibility options** include the following settings.

Keyboard:

'StickyKeys' is mainly for one-handed use by allowing the use of Shift or Ctrl keys with a single press rather than pressing them simultaneously with another key.

'Filterkeys' screens out repeated key strokes for users who find it hard to lift their fingers off the keyboard.

'ToggleKeys' makes sounds when keys such as Caps Lock are pressed.

Sound includes 'Sound Sentry' which makes a sound when a message comes up on screen, and 'Show sounds' to display captions for sounds the computer makes.

Display will change the appearance of the screen, for instance to a high contrast black screen with large, white icons.

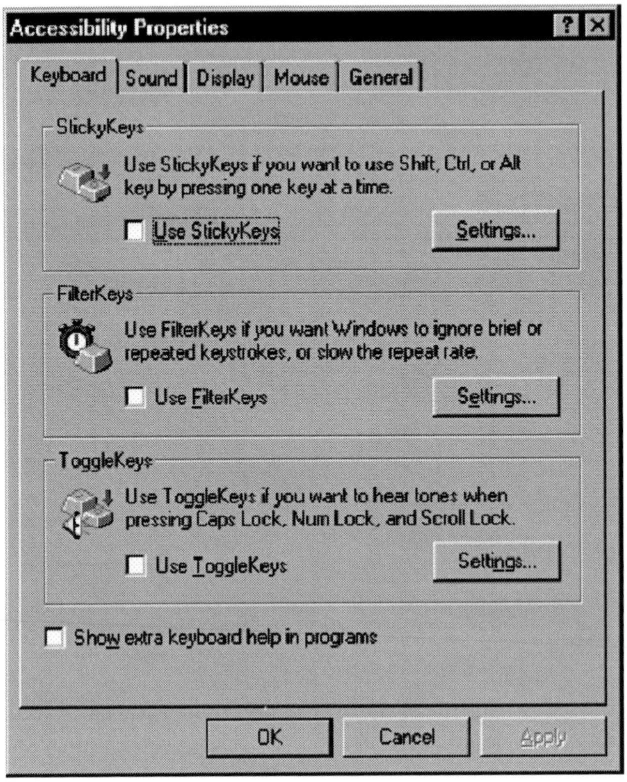

Figure 2.2 *Accessibility options*

The **Mouse** tab lets you control the mouse with the numeric pad of the keyboard and the **General** tab lets you specify how long the accessibility features should be left on for.

However, these are not the only adjustments to be made through the **Control Panel**. The **Mouse** controls include swapping the buttons for left-handed users, changing the double-click speed, changing the size and colour of the arrow, and adding trails to make it easier to follow.

It is also possible to change the appearance of the screen through the **Display** options. This is useful for people who find certain colour combinations easier to read. By clicking on the **Appearance** tab and then the **Advanced** button you will be able to change the colour of all windows, both background and text. This means, for instance, that Microsoft Word could appear with a pink page and blue text, although when printed it will still be black on white. This facility is particularly helpful for some people with dyslexia.

There are several other ways in which word processors in particular can be adapted to make them more suitable for pupils with SEN. These are covered in the section on word-processing.

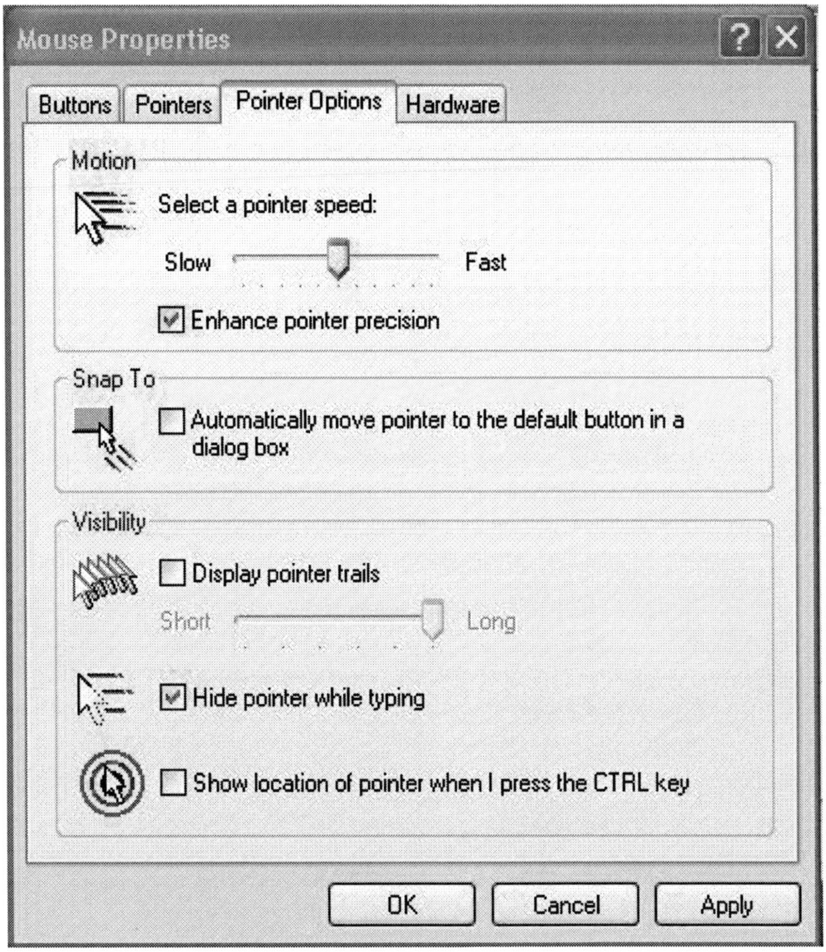

Figure 2.3 *Mouse properties dialog box*

Adding to what you already have

There are two things we can add to a computer: more hardware and more software. The first generally makes physical access easier, the second can also make tasks easier.

A computer is ordinarily set up with a keyboard, a monitor and a mouse. We can change any of these to make the machine easier to use. We could, for instance, make the monitor larger so that the screen is easier to see (although for some pupils with visual impairments even this may not help as their field of vision may be limited to a small area).

Another adaptation would be to use a touch screen monitor. As the name suggests, these are activated by touching. The use of this technology is becoming very common, when buying rail or tube tickets for instance, or for information points in museums. Like ordinary monitors, they come either as a standard type or as a flat screen. There are also screens that clip on to existing monitors to add this functionality.

Figure 2.4 *Advanced Appearance dialog box*

Figure 2.5 *Touch screen*

Alternative keyboards come in several forms. One easy adaptation is to add a key guard. This is usually a sheet of pressed metal with finger-sized holes drilled into it which clips over a standard keyboard. This is for users with poor motor control so that they can run their hand over the guard then press down through the hole to select a key, preventing them from making multiple presses.

Figure 2.6 *Big Keys keyboard*

The Big Keys range have just that, bigger keys that are easier to find and to see. They come in various formats: upper or lower case; qwerty or alphabetical; black on white or coloured keys; and also take a key guard.

Other keyboards change the shape, so that it is no longer flat, for greater flexibility of positioning.

Another variation is the concept keyboard, one of the most popular of which is the Intellikeys.

Figure 2.7 *Intellikeys*

This has a flat surface which can be angled, on which overlays can be inserted. In some ways the concept keyboard is not a direct replacement for the standard keyboard as it can also be used to control any element of the computer, such as the mouse, and is therefore not just for writing text. The overlays may look like a standard keyboard, or just have arrows to drive the mouse, or may even be specially constructed to look like the software on screen. They are operated by pressing with a finger or a pointing device and can be positioned for optimal control by the user with the overlays changed simply by slipping one out and another in. A bar code reader on the back tells the computer which one is in use.

Alternatives to the standard mouse generally work by turning it upside down. Usually the user moves the mouse around the mat and this moves the ball underneath. With mouse alternatives this is reversed: the mouse stays still and the user controls the ball directly. This is clear with a tracker ball such as the Kidtrac. It is also true for joysticks. While these look like the ones used for gaming, they are generally more robust (and do not have buttons to fire missiles or accelerate cars). Other variations include smaller tracker balls designed to be rolled with minimum movement of one finger and touch pads like those used on laptops.

Figure 2.8 *Tracker*

Figure 2.9 *Joystick*

Apart from these devices, which are variations on the ways we already use computers, there are other hardware adaptations that can require us to think differently about how we operate it. A commonly used device is the 'Switch' which quite often looks like a button. These devices vary in sophistication both in their design and their use. The basis of it is that by hitting the switch an action occurs. Some users will be learning cause and effect, perhaps that the action causes a pattern to build on screen. Others will be using one or more switches in various ways to select letters and words to build up texts or to control their computers. The system used by Professor Stephen Hawking to write his books is essentially a switch-driven one.

Figure 2.10 *Switch*

Switches can also be used with varying degrees of complexity to work communication aids. These can vary from a single button with a pre-recorded message, such as 'Here, Miss' to be used at registration, through rows of messages to be worked with a direct press or through scanning with a switch, to those that have several levels and allow users to hold complex conversations.

When considering specialist hardware and software for pupils, the help of other professionals should be enlisted. Occupational or speech therapists can advise on positioning and use of technology, and some local education authorities (LEAs) also have specialist teachers to do this. In many instances, common sense will guide you, but it will be as well to ask an expert as sometimes positioning of equipment can lead to longer-term health problems.

Specialist software

Some additional hardware also requires specialised software. Switch users may need particular programs in order to get the hang of how they work. These might work by building a pattern, as in 'Switch It! Patterns' or a familiar object as in

'Switch It! Diggers'. Other titles such as 'Choose It Maker' are designed for switch use and can also teach concepts such as sequencing.

For pupils learning to use touch screens or tracker balls, painting programs are a useful starting point as they give immediate results and will work in a similar way to painting on paper.

Pupils who rely on keyboards will benefit from learning how to use them properly. While touch typing is a highly desirable skill, the constraints of the timetable and the fact that this can be a very boring pursuit might prevent it happening. However, familiarity with the keyboard will speed up writing. Programs such as 'Type to Learn' try to strike a balance between the repetitiveness of learning and the use of games to brighten things up. There are also specialist programs such as 'Five Fingered Typist' for those who will only use one hand.

It is known that developing a motor memory of how words are spelt can help pupils with literacy difficulties or dyslexia. By regularly building words on a keyboard the movement of fingers helps pupils to remember how to spell them. This is recognised in 'First Keys to Literacy' which teaches children initial letter sounds and simple spellings alongside keyboard awareness.

Perhaps the most common use of a computer is to create texts and there are lots of different ways in which software can support this. One that is becoming quite familiar is the use of prediction software. This is widely used for text messaging on mobile phones: as the user's thumbs tap away so suggestions are made as to the word they may be wanting to use. Computer versions, such as 'Penfriend' and 'Co:Writer', work in a similar way. The user types in the first letter and a list of words appears. If the desired one is not there, they can add another letter and so on until the word they want appears – or does not. Although even then these programs will learn new words and add them into the store of those available ready for the next time. Selection can be by using the mouse or by pressing a key, often the Function keys at the top of the keyboard.

Predictive software is useful for pupils who have difficulty spelling, as they only need to begin to spell the word and then pick it out from a list, and for those with motor control difficulties. For this latter group, this software reduces the number of keystrokes necessary to write any word. As the predictor will often suggest the next word without any letters being given, this can mean writing a whole sentence with just one click of the mouse for each word.

Another common support for pupils when writing is the use of word grids. These can provide individual words, phrases or whole sentences which can be added to the text by the click of a mouse or by pressing a switch. There are specialist programs for this, the most well known of which is 'Clicker 4' and its variant for secondary pupils 'Wordbar'. This is also a feature of other software such as 'Talking First Word' and 'Softease Studio'.

The advantage of using programs with word grids is that support can be given to pupils in several ways at several levels. 'Clicker 4' can be set to be simply an on-screen keyboard, or it can give difficult words or key vocabulary to be used alongside typing, or it can be used to create whole texts through given sentences and phrases. Some children can use it to sequence a known text, others as a personalised vocabulary book. At another level it can also be used to create talking books and multimedia presentations.

In this grid, designed for Year 1 pupils, a writing frame has been created for procedural writing about making breakfast.

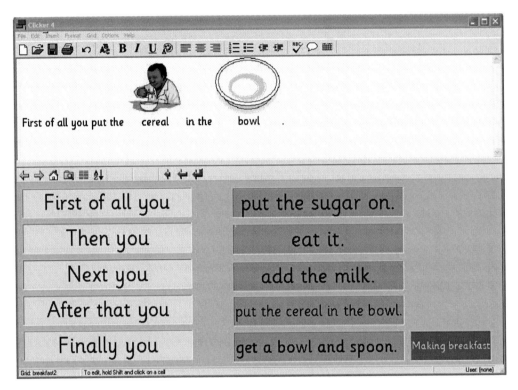

Figure 2.11 *A Clicker Grid for writing about making breakfast*

This is one of six grids, each offering a different menu. Others include making a milkshake or having a piece of toast. Another feature of 'Clicker 4' is that it can be set to show graphics for words that are in its database of images. This can be set to work with either the grids or the writing area. Other images, such as photos of children, can be added as well. A grid-based spellchecker will include images when the writing is checked for accuracy.

'Clicker 4' comes with its own talking word processor built in. This can be set to read letters, words, sentences or words that are clicked. This is also true of other talking word processors such as 'Talking Write Away', 'Talking First Word', 'Write Outloud' and 'Texthelp'.

A talking word processor offers support by reading back what the user has just typed in. At letter level this can be useful to visually impaired typists who need to know that they are accurate. However, as it is the letter name rather than the sound that is given, it is of limited value for those starting to learn to spell. At word level the computer will read the input phonetically, so 'kow' or 'kat' will sound correct.

With the use of graphics, as in 'Clicker 4' the additional support of a picture will let the pupil know when these spellings are correct. When the computer reads the whole sentence the user will be able hear whether it makes sense, if the words are in the right order and if any have been missed out.

Talking word processors are also useful for reading out whole passages of text. There are also programs specifically designed as screen readers, such as 'Screen Reader' from Lorien Systems.

Another support for reading is the use of symbols. Although the most widely used of such programs is 'Writing with Symbols 2000' (WWS2K), one of its key uses is to help pupils make the link between words and the concepts that they represent.

Figure 2.12 *A screenshot of Writing with Symbols 2000*

Whether creating text and seeing symbols appear to represent its meaning or using the program to decode existing writing, it is a very powerful way of making literacy accessible for a wide range of pupils. A number of different symbol sets can be used and additional graphics, such as photos, added. The company that produce it, Widgit, also make 'Intercomm' for using symbols with email and in the spring of 2004 they introduced a symbol-based web-browser.

Other more specialist software includes those designed as on-screen keyboards such as 'Wivik' and 'Wordwall'. Both of these put a keyboard on screen which the user points at then either clicks or simply 'dwells' on. Selection of a letter brings up a list from a predictor. 'Wordwall' is part of a suite called 'The Grid' with which the user can control all the functions of the computer.

This level of control is also available from some of the more sophisticated speech to text programs such as 'Dragon Dictate'. As well as writing the text, the user can give commands including opening programs, formatting text, saving and printing. As they have developed so these programs have become more reliable and are now said to be as accurate as typing. The only drawback is that users currently need to have a reading age of around 12 to be able to recognise and correct any wrong words the computer types. It is possible to have the program read back the text, but there is still the issue of dictating in a corrected spelling.

The use of ICT to ameliorate SEN continues to develop. The possibility already exists to control the mouse through pads attached to the forehead picking up minute electrical impulses. Beyond this it is possible to wire the nervous system directly into a machine and there is work in the United States on using the power of thought to control the computer directly. All the time the gap between the machine and the brain is narrowing. The closer the link, the greater will be the possibilities for users with SEN to exploit the power of the technology.

Supporting pupils with English as an Additional Language (EAL)

Pupils who are learning English in addition to their mother tongue will be acquiring the skills of literacy alongside the English language itself with all its various nuances, subtleties and inconsistencies. ICT can offer help in many ways.

One support is in reading out loud to children. There are lots of talking books on the market, many for younger children although secondary-age course books are becoming more common. These will read the text, usually highlighting the words on screen, and many offer additional tools such as meanings or criticism of the text. Several titles from the ever popular Oxford Reading Tree are available, as well as more entertainment-orientated titles such as 'Arthur's Teacher Trouble' from Broderbund. At secondary level there is the 'Start to Finish' range from Don Johnson.

A lot of the supports offered by ICT for pupils with SEN can be used for children with EAL. 'Writing with Symbols 2000' immediately offers a bridge between the text and the concept it represents. Likewise the speech and graphic support of 'Clicker 4' will support developing independence as learners type in words and receive reinforcement. The use of word grids can also help with the creation of exercises such as matching words with their meanings.

Another useful tool is the use of cloze exercises, where words are missed out of a text for pupils to complete. 'Clozepro' comes from Crick, the same firm that produces 'Clicker 4', and can be used in a similar way. A reading passage is created and pupils use a grid to complete it. However, it can be configured differently so that users have to select from a drop-down list or even simply type it in. As these exercises can be created quite quickly, they can be used to check pupils' understanding of language in several ways, both in choosing the word as well as the part of speech.

There are also tools to help pupils explore the English language. The 'Visual Thesaurus' offers networks of links between words along with their meanings, which operate on more than one plain so they appear to be 3D. This could be used to explore language, discussing the different choices and how and when each might be used.

Another way of exploring language is through the Internet. There are now a number of sites offering translation. These tend to be between languages with

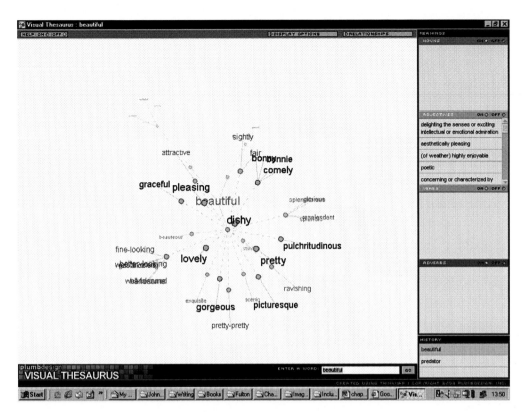

Figure 2.13 *The Visual Thesaurus appears to be 3D*

commercial links for international business, so Russian and Arabic might be offered but not Bengali or Urdu. Typing in a word or phrase in one language will bring a translation into the other. The best known of these is 'Babelfish' which includes Chinese, Russian and Korean among its offerings. Google offers 'Language Tools' on its front page but these are mainly between European languages.

Another useful tool to be found on the Internet is 'Banglaword'. This is a Bengali word processor that uses a Western keyboard and phonetics to create Bengali scripts. Many young Bengalis can read their mother tongue but not accurately write it. This software will allow them to write in their mother tongue using their knowledge of English.

Gifted and talented pupils

This group of pupils often explore the ICT on offer simply to see what it will do (and to see if they can make it do something it should not). Such energies need to be directed into creative tasks. Computers can offer both more challenging tasks and more challenge in how the task is completed.

There are many ways in which ICT can be used to extend tasks. Excel, for instance, can be used in maths to explore complex calculations and to look for patterns, or to draw graphs of mathematical expressions. Pupils can also change the different types of charts to see how they each represent something different.

Using MSWord can present a number of challenges. Under the **Tools** menu is a **Word count**. This can be used to challenge pupils to write to a specific length. A task might be to create a complete story in under 100 words or retell a Shakespeare play in exactly 50 words. Also under the **Tools** menu is the **Language** tool where you will find the **Thesaurus** (this is also available in later versions by **Right clicking** on a word and choosing **Synonyms**). Children can be challenged to use this to find more interesting descriptive words. Change 'walked' to 'ambled' or 'paced', or maybe 'smiled' to 'smirked' or 'beamed'.

The use of some software can lead these pupils to create their own challenges in learning how it works. 'PowerPoint', for instance, has many variations of animations and transitions. The presentations themselves can offer pupils opportunities to show their skills through the complexity of what they produce. Other tasks, such as creating web pages, in themselves can be quite demanding. Programs such as 'Logo' are open-ended in the degree of challenge available, from creating sequences of squares to having the turtle write their name in joined-up writing.

The Internet offers an enormous resource of information, allowing pupils to pursue their interests to a greater depth. One way of doing this is through the use of webquests. In these pupils are asked to complete specific jobs and often take on a particular role – advertising executive for holidays to Mars, for instance, or catering manager for the spacecraft to take them there. In this instance the task may be the same across the class but the more able can be expected to produce a more considered outcome.

Offering new opportunities

One of the reasons why a computer is such a powerful tool for learning is the new opportunities it makes available. As the term 'Information and Communication Technology' implies, the possibilities are not only in the resources that it makes available but also in the new ways of communication on offer.

ICT helps any of us to create publications, reports and documents that at the very least look professional. These tools are breaking down barriers to creativity and achievement by giving us the resources to do things for ourselves that previously only highly skilled professionals could do, such as laying out pages for printing or editing movies. It also makes available sources of information that were previously only available to a restricted few.

Original census data from the end of the nineteenth century is now online – a rich, primary source for studying history, geography, statistics, sociology, economics and politics at many levels. We can find maps and aerial photos of many places in the world and on some sites overlay one with the other. Photos and film of historic events, scientific advances or faraway places, such as Mars, are easily available.

The use of web cams allows us to both receive information and to give it out. There are cameras pointed at watering holes and nesting places around the world for us to see animals in their natural habitat. There are times when nothing can be seen because animals often water at dawn and dusk when people are not in school. This may be what children then learn.

Web cams also offer rudimentary videoconferencing. While the images can be poor quality, the opportunity to both see and talk to someone can create a richer learning experience. Better quality videoconferencing equipment is leading to all sorts of learning situations. This might be one expert addressing schools across a wide geographical area, or similarly students sharing their experiences. One such project links the Shetland Islands to South Africa for a higher level course on the Apartheid system. The Global Leap website links up schools with providers of conferences to give learning experiences that were hitherto impossible.

Even more everyday facilities, such as email, can open up learning. One example is sending Amelia Bear around the world. This stuffed toy is visiting schools who then send messages about what she has discovered and photos of her in the places she has visited. You might be able to set up something similar for your pupils through friends or relatives living abroad, or former supply teachers who have returned to far-flung locations.

There has been discussion about how such uses of ICT will change classrooms so that pupils can be supervised by teaching assistants while taught from a far by subject experts. While this might seem attractive, the richest learning experiences arise from the educational professionals working alongside pupils to tailor learning to the needs of individuals and groups. ICT can really enrich learning for pupils regardless of their individual learning needs.

The range of hardware and software available might seem daunting and it would be very difficult to know how to use it all. It is therefore better to know a handful of programs well and use them effectively than to know a little about a lot. Focus on being able to find and use appropriate software for the pupils you work with for the tasks they need to complete (see 3-17.2,e,f).

PART 2

ICT in the classroom

CHAPTER 3

Using ICT in teaching and learning

ICT is both a curriculum subject and a tool for learning in other subjects. It can be seen, like handwriting, as a 'service subject', one that enables learning. The skills learnt in ICT lessons are put into practice in other areas of the curriculum.

The National Curriculum breaks ICT down into several strands under two common headings: 'Knowledge, Skills and Understanding' and 'Breadth of Study'. The first of these is what children should learn, the latter the learning experiences they should encounter in the process.

The ICT curriculum has four aspects:

● Finding things out

● Developing ideas and making things happen

● Exchanging and sharing information

● Reviewing, modifying and evaluating work as it progresses

These themes are developed over the four key stages; however, the broad aims are consistent throughout a pupil's schooling. How these are delivered through the curriculum is up to schools; however, a scheme of work has been provided by the Qualifications and Curriculum Authority (QCA), and by initiatives such as the Key Stage 3 ICT Strategy. It is not compulsory for schools to follow these, but whatever is taught should be at least as good as the QCA standard.

There are a number of key activities that ICT is used for in the school curriculum. These include:

● Creating and revising text

● Creating and revising graphics

- Combining text and graphics

- Collecting and analysing data

- Performing calculations

- Modelling situations and answering 'what if' questions

- Controlling real and virtual machines

- Combining text, graphics, sound and video

- Creating presentations to communicate ideas

- Finding information

- Communicating electronically

Common tasks will include: writing stories and adding pictures, perhaps as a class newspaper; programming a robot to complete a course; analysing the costs of a small business; creating a multimedia presentation about the school environment; and comparing the weather around the world.

Quite often the software to complete all these tasks will come as one package, a suite of programs, perhaps termed a 'toolkit', such as those from Granada, Black Cat and 2Simple. However, the most common toolkit in use in schools is not one created for pupils, but for businesses and homes – MS Office. The next section will look at the various programs in this suite and the ways in which they can be used with pupils, including adapting them, making use of their functions and some ideas for activities with pupils.

CHAPTER 4

Using a word processor

Creating texts of various types is probably the most widely used function of a computer in schools. It is a very powerful tool as it allows us to revise and edit until the text says just what we want it to. Other tools mean that everyone is now able to produce professional-looking documents; we can alter the appearance in a number of ways so that not just the words but also the presentation appear highly polished.

However, most word processors are designed for literate, adult users who know what they want to say and for whom the in-built tools are a support. For pupils with developing literacy skills these packages may need a bit of tweaking.

Writing with a word processor

The act of writing is fairly complicated as we do a number of things simultaneously. We decide on the words that will express our thoughts and the order they need to go in. We spell them selecting the letters that make them up and, if writing by hand, form the letters that make the words, moving the pen accurately across the paper. We also think about the technical elements of grammar, putting the pauses and the emphases in places that give sense to the strings of words. It is not surprising, then, that this task can seem daunting.

With a word processor the task can be staged, broken down into components, to make it much more manageable. Pupils can put down words then read them through afterwards, adding more or reassembling until they get the sense they want, gradually building the structure of the piece. They can spell things pretty much as they want then take time to get the letters in the correct order. Forming the letters properly is done for them by the machine, which offers a large number of styles, or fonts, to choose from. Punctuation can also be added at the end, perhaps as the child reads it through aloud and gets the sense of where it needs to be. By providing a structure for creating the text in stages, a difficult task becomes much more doable.

An example of this is the writing of a haiku. Haikus appear in the National Literacy Strategy in Term 3 of Year 4. This is quite a sophisticated form of poetry, originally from Japan, that imposes certain disciplines on the writer and can be fairly challenging. It is made up of three lines, the first of five syllables, the second seven and the last another five. Ideally the first line introduces one idea, the second brings in another, then the third brings them together. There are other rules, such as including a reference to a season, but these are not always followed in school. While this may sound difficult, it lends itself to a very structured approach. The method shown below is one I first heard of in a Year 8 class.

How to write a haiku

1. Make a list (i.e. each word on a new line) of ten words to do with trees.

2. Develop a sentence for each word (Note: the word can be anywhere in the sentence).

3. Choose three sentences you like and delete the rest (or save them into a new document if you think you might want to write another one or cannot bear destroying your creative thoughts).

4. Cut and paste the remaining sentences into a pleasing order.

5. Edit line one to five syllables.

6. Edit line two to seven syllables.

7. Edit line three to five syllables.

8. Now think about presentation. Choose a suitable font (such as *Lucida Handwriting*) and change its size and the line spacing (see below) and the alignment.

9. Add some clip art.

10. Give it a title and add a name and date.

11. Print it out and put it on the wall.

In this example the structure of the work was determined by the teacher, however; planning always helps. As a general rule the steps are:

- Plan – Often best done away from the computer through techniques such as brainstorming and mind-mapping with pencil and paper.

- Write – Get the words down.

- Edit – Reorder the words, check the spelling, correct the punctuation.

- Publish – Whether as a printout for the teacher to mark, as part of a class display or as a web page with the world as its audience, it is important that children's creative efforts are acknowledged.

Making the word processor pupil-friendly

There are a number of tools built in to computer programs that are designed to be supportive and to make the job easier. Often these do the opposite.

You are probably familiar with many of these automatic functions: green and red wavy lines under your text, capital letters that pop into place, words that automatically rewrite themselves (type 'adn' and 'and' will pop up in its place). While a useful prop for people whose fingers slip, these can be an off-putting distraction for pupils.

In the haiku example, for instance, the computer may well have given each new word in the list a capital letter. This is one of the tools from the 'Autocorrect' menu along with capitalising the first letter of days of the week. These are not necessarily helpful unless children already know when to use capitals.

To turn these tools off, open **Tools>Autocorrect>** and uncheck the appropriate boxes.

Uncheck these boxes.

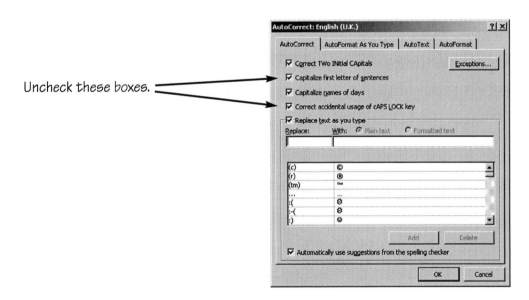

Figure 4.1 *Autocorrect options*

Unfortunately not all these options are in the same place. To stop MS Word automatically inserting dates, and greetings such as 'yours truly', you need to follow **Insert>Autotext**; click on the **Autotext** Tab and uncheck the 'Show Autocomplete Suggestions' box.

Spellcheckers can be false friends. Apart from decorating the page with wavy

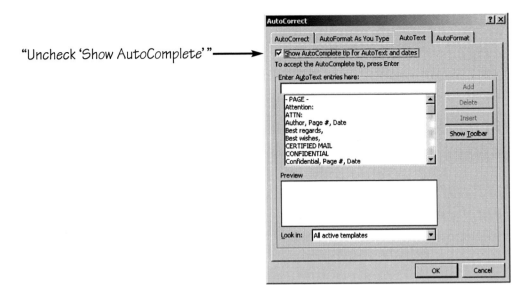

"Uncheck 'Show AutoComplete' "

Figure 4.2 *Autocomplete*

red lines, they do not work with the sense of a sentence but on mathematical principles. The computer compares the set of letters with a database and suggests the nearest grouping rather than the one that makes sense. In some instances the word is not in the database, such as some peoples' names; in others pupils may accept the first word suggested not because it is correct but because of a belief that the computer is smarter than they are when it comes to spelling.

As for grammar checkers, I am never sure what it is that I might have done wrong, so I am not convinced the pupils will know either.

To turn off automatic spelling and grammar checking, open **Tools>Options> Spelling & Grammar** then uncheck 'Check spelling as you type' and 'Check grammar as you type'.

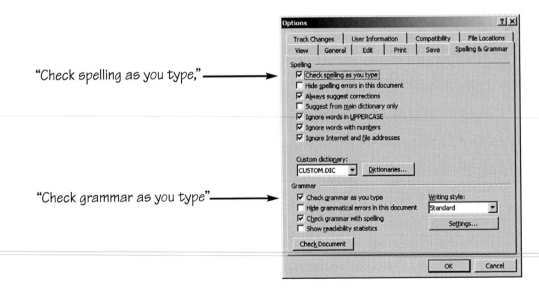

"Check spelling as you type,"

"Check grammar as you type"

Figure 4.3 *Spelling and grammar options*

As a general rule it is better to check spellings on a printout than on screen. This means that the pupils will get the text down without distraction and it allows you to limit the number of words to be checked, for instance to key vocabulary or high frequency words. It will also give opportunities for dictionary work.

In fact it is preferable to do any final editing on a hard copy – a printout – as we sometimes miss on screen what is obvious on paper. It is something we will all have experienced and yet nobody knows why it happens. To make editing and, indeed, reading easier, a couple of other changes to how MS Word is set up are necessary.

Changing appearances

As a general rule text is easier to read if the text size is large and the writing spread out. The font size should be in the order of 14 to 18 points, and the line spacing 1.5 or double. We also need to choose fonts that are easy to read. The majority of fonts use a lower case letter 'A' (a), for instance, that looks like an upside down 'G' (g). For most children this causes no problems, but for some it adds to the confusion of decoding. Comic Sans has correctly formed letters, as does the Sassoon family of fonts, developed to support young children's development of writing skills. However, some fonts, such as 𝔒𝔩𝔡𝔢 𝔈𝔫𝔤𝔩𝔦𝔰𝔥 can make it hard work for anyone to make sense of the text.

You can change the font style and size for every new document quite easily. Open **Format>Font** then select a new font and size and click on the 'Default' button.

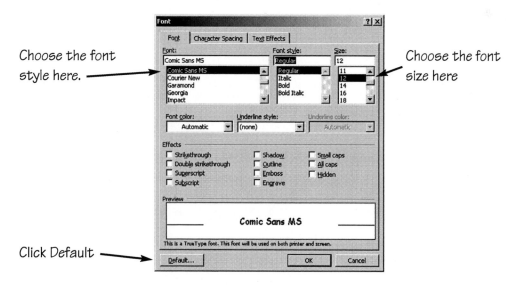

Figure 4.4 *Changing font size and style*

When the dialogue box asks you, 'Do you want to change the font to (Default) Comic Sans MS? This will affect all new documents based on the NORMAL Template', click **Yes.**

Changing the line spacing is straightforward. However, permanently changing it is less so as it requires replacing the 'Normal' template. (What this means will become clearer in the next section.) To increase the line spacing, follow **Format>Paragraph** then click on 'Line Spacing' and increase it to '1.5 lines' or 'Double', then click 'OK'.

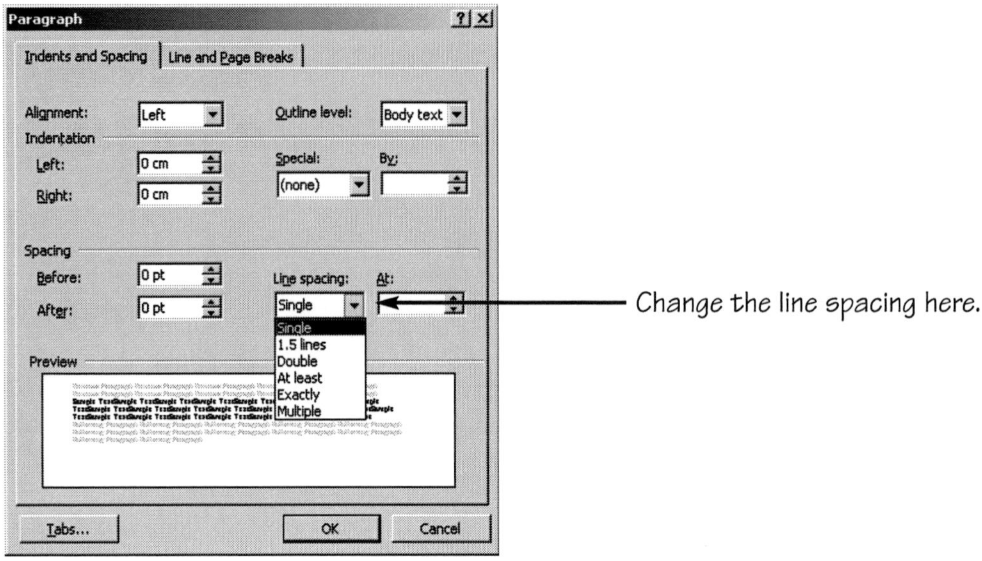

Figure 4.5 *Changing line spacing*

The word processor as a tool for learning

So far we have looked at how we can use MS Word to structure writing and modify existing tools to make it more useful for our pupils. There are also tools we can create for pupils to use.

Templates

A template is a document that remains unchanged in its original format when it is opened and worked on. It allows for many users to use the same document.

In writing, for instance, it is often helpful to provide pupils with a 'Writing Frame'. This generally takes the form of a number of sentence starters structured to develop the writing. A piece of instructional writing might read:

You will need . . .

First you . . .

Then you . . .

Next . . .

After that . . .

Finally . . .

In Key Stage 1 this might take the form of 'How to make a jam sandwich':

You will need bread, butter, jam, a knife and a plate.

First you wash your hands.

Then you put the butter on the bread.

Next you add the jam.

After that you put the bread together.

Finally you eat it.

While this is very simple, it helps children to structure their writing. It could be used in secondary school to write up an investigation perhaps.

Creating a template is straightforward:

1. Type in the structure you want pupils to use.

2. Save it as a template.

3. Close it.

4. Start working on it.

When you have first created your document and are saving it, just change the 'Save as type' box to 'Template' and the computer will automatically put it with the other templates available.

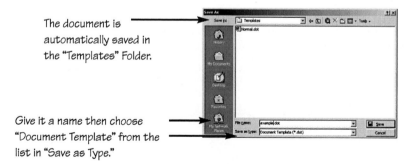

The document is automatically saved in the "Templates" Folder.

Give it a name then choose "Document Template" from the list in "Save as Type."

Figure 4.6 *Saving as a template*

To use the template simply follow **File>new** then choose the template you created from the list presented.

Word processors used for reading

While we mostly write with a word processor, with a little bit of thought we can make quite creative reading activities too. This extract is from 'The Pied Piper of Hamelin' by Robert Browning.

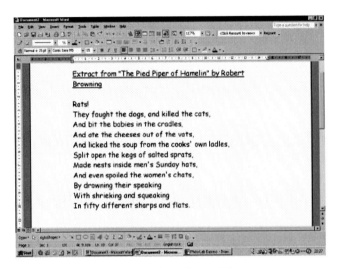

Figure 4.7 *A reading activity*

We might want children to focus on the rhyming scheme. Using the 'Bold', 'Underline' and 'Italic' tools we can ask them to pick it out. It might look like this.

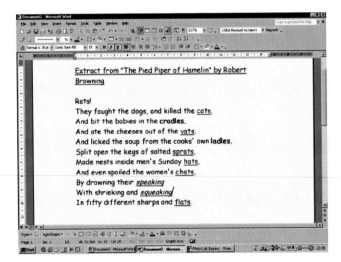

Figure 4.8 *Use of bold, underline and italic*

Or we could use the **Highlighter** tool to create a multicoloured version like this.

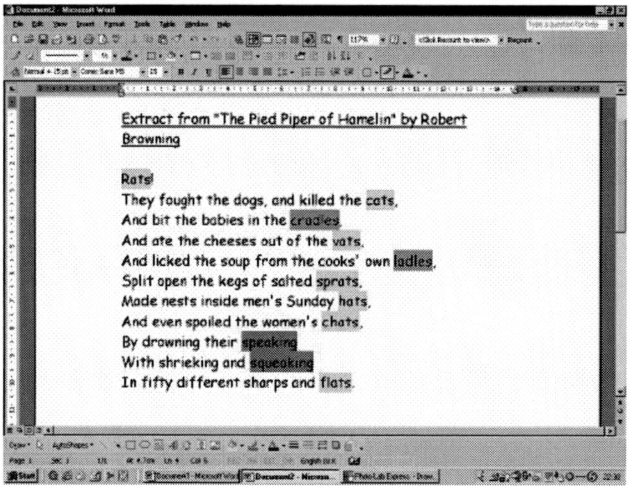

Figure 4.9 *Use of highlighting*

Finally we might just want to look for all the words that rhyme with 'Rats'. To do this we might simply delete everything else.

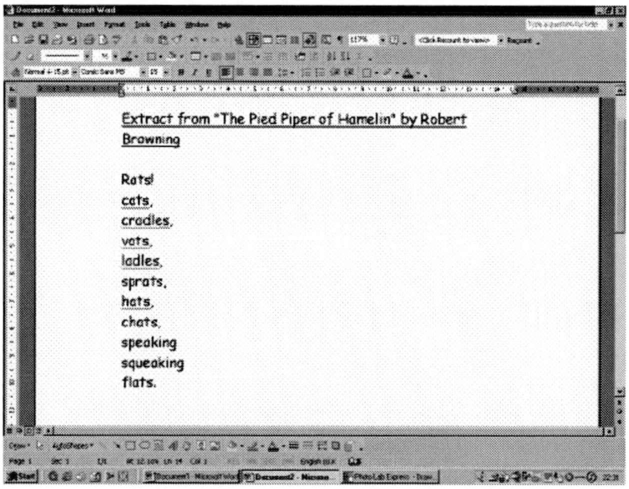

Figure 4.10 *Non-rhyming words deleted*

These processes will also work at secondary level. Again we could pick out the rhyming scheme of a poem, or we might use it for an exercise in reading for information. Here Shakespeare's 'Seven Ages of Man' have been reduced to a simple list by deleting everything else.

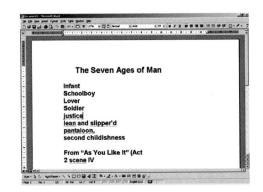

Figure 4.11 *The seven ages of man with words deleted*

(Note: When you first start working on a new document you are using a template called 'Normal'. To change the way this is set up, you need to create a new file and save it with another name – 'New normal' perhaps. Then exit MS Word and use Windows Explorer to find the folder where templates are kept. Next delete the 'Normal' template and rename 'New normal' as 'Normal'. If this seems daunting, find 'The one who knows' and she or he will gladly do it for you.)

Other tools

There are a few other tools that can be adapted to support pupils, including some of those we might previously have turned off.

Autocorrect is the feature that automatically replaces one, usually misspelt, word with another, for instance 'teh' with 'the'. This can be made to work to children's advantage by reducing key strokes. For instance, a pupil's initials can be substituted by full name and class on the press of the space bar.

Type the code here. →

← Type the text here.

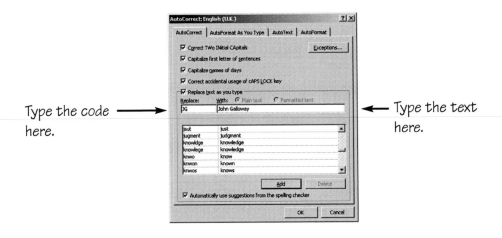

Figure 4.12 *The autocorrect dialog box*

This is particularly useful for pupils with fine motor control difficulties.

Autotext is a similar feature that replaces a code with given text except that it is not automatic and requires the user to press F3 to activate it.

Another useful tool is the **Word Count** found in the **Tools** menu. This can provide a useful challenge to all pupils. For instance, pupils might be asked to write the opening for a horror story establishing the setting and main characters in exactly 50 words. Some pupils may find the challenge is in writing so many words, others in writing so few.

Galloway's rules of word-processing

The word processor is a powerful tool, but consideration needs to be given to its use. Here are some thoughts for your guidance.

- Plan before you start writing.
- Write directly onto the computer, do not copy out from a draft book as this undermines the power of the word processor.
- Do not worry about spelling mistakes until the first draft is written. Turn off distracting spelling and grammar checkers and do not let pupils use spellcheckers unsupervised.
- Use a simple font with a size of at least 14 points and at least 1.5 line spacing.
- Do the final editing on a hard copy.
- The pupils do not always have to do the typing.
- Exploit the possibilities for collaboration.

Beyond the obvious advantages of using a word processor given in this chapter, there are several less text-orientated benefits. Computers can be great motivators that increase concentration and raise self-esteem. They allow all pupils to produce work that at the very least looks professional. As a tool for group work and collaboration, they allow several people to work on one piece, either through simply seeing the screen or by sharing work through electronic communication.

And finally computers have endless patience, allowing us to work and rework until we are satisfied. It will never get tired of us, even if we get tired of it. If this happens, remember who controls the 'Off' switch, and use it.

CHAPTER 5

Using a desktop publisher

Desktop publishing (DTP) packages give you more flexibility when creating documents than word processors. When using the latter the text starts at the top of the page and moves down as you add more or hit the return key. You can, of course, add images, colour and borders but the positioning of these are largely governed by the block of writing. With a DTP you have much more flexibility about where everything sits on the page and how it all works together.

Whether creating worksheets to use in lessons, or working alongside the pupils to create publications such as newsletters and greetings cards, you will find that this is a powerful tool which will allow you to create work of a professional standard. Increasingly teaching assistants are supporting children by working outside of the classroom making resources and tailoring them to particular groups or individuals. Whatever you are making, these programs will enable you to do it to the highest standard.

Things to remember when using DTP

Because they do not work as other programs do, it is important to remember a few keys points, mainly that you have to select the tool you want to use for the element of the page you are working on, and that when you do the menus and toolbars will change accordingly. So if you choose the **Text Tool**, the menus and toolbars will become those of a word processor. Here are a few things worth remembering:

- Everything placed on the page is an 'object', whether it is text, image, table or heading.

- Select the tool to create the type of object you want from the selection on the left of the screen.

- Create the area you want that object to fill on your document by placing the cross-hairs cursor at one corner, hold down the left mouse button, then pull to the opposite corner (they are easy to resize, move or delete as you refine your creation).

- The toolbar and menus at the top of the screen change depending on which type of object you are working with.

- You will know which object is 'active' because it will have black or white squares at each corner and on the middle of each side. These are the 'handles' with which you can resize it.

- To edit an existing object, double click on it. The handles will appear and the menus and toolbars will change.

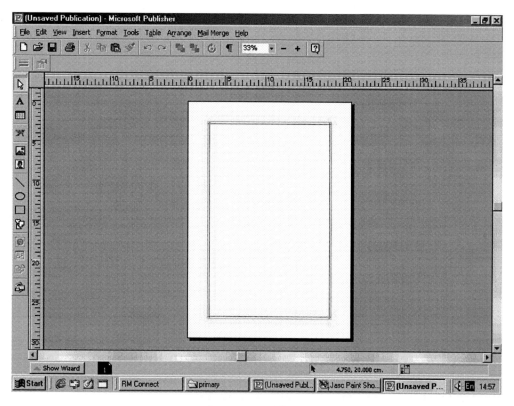

Figure 5.1 *A full page*

On this fresh page in MS Publisher no objects have been created. The **Pointer** tool is chosen and the basic commands are shown at the top. To choose another tool you simply click on it from the selection on the left and the cursor will change to cross hairs ready to create a fresh object. The pink and blue lines in the middle are just guides, not limits to where you can work. Either ignore them or get rid of them by following **View>Page guides.**

$+$

Figure 5.2 *The cross-hairs cursor*

With most of the tools, it is obvious what they do, for example the shapes create that shape, the **Table Frame** tool will insert a table. The **Clip Art** and **Picture Frame** tools both insert images, the first from the gallery of graphics provided with the program, the second from another source such as digital photos or pictures drawn on the computer or scanned in. Two tools are available to create text: **WordArt** for headings and labels, and **Text Frame** for the 'story'.

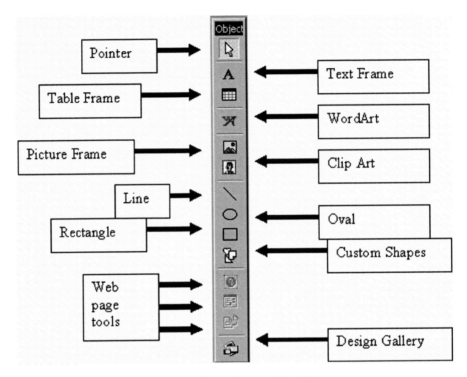

Figure 5.3 *The toolbar in MS Publisher*

When you first start MS Publisher it offers you a range of formats for documents and three ways to create them.

Publications by wizard walks you through the process, asking you to provide information that is automatically placed in a completed publication which you can then edit.

Publications by design offers the same range of publications with certain design features, such as colour scheme, font and layout, already selected.

Blank publications arranges the layout for your creation but leaves everything else to you. As you can see from the screenshot below, a number of formats for publications are on offer including cards, banners, posters and web pages.

All of these can be printed on A4 paper then trimmed or glued together to make the finished product.

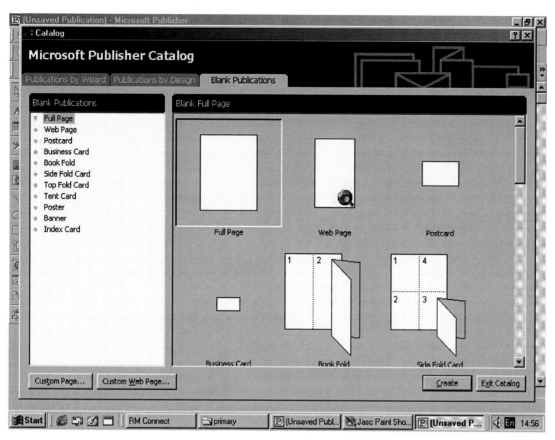

Figure 5.4 *The blank publications*

Making a greetings card

This is a useful format not only for making cards for pupils to give to people, but also to create four-page books – or eight pages if you put one inside another. Three formats are available: side fold, top fold and tent fold – all self-explanatory. Double-clicking on any one of these brings up a prompt asking if you want to automatically insert pages. If you say 'Yes', the computer creates a four-page publication that will print on one sheet of A4 and fold down into your chosen card. The number of pages will be displayed at the bottom of the screen like this.

Figure 5.5 *Page selection*

Clicking on a number will take you to that page.

Creating a greetings card is a useful introduction to DTP for both yourselves and your pupils. It will need you to use **WordArt** for a heading, such as 'Happy Holiday', **Clip Art** for an image on the front and **Text** for the message on the inside. You may also decide to add coloured backgrounds and borders to any of these.

If you are teaching others, it is best to show them the whole process then go back and repeat it step by step with them following you. An interactive whiteboard is ideal for this but, depending on the size of the group, a large monitor might be sufficient.

Before you start, introduce the task so that they can be thinking of a greeting while you are instructing them. There is usually a suitable event at any time in the year – if Diwali, Eid, Mother's Day or Easter are too far off there is always 'Thank you for being my friend' or 'Happy Friday'. Begin by choosing one of the card types and opening it. You may find that the left of the screen is filled by an offer from the program to start a 'Wizard' to guide you. Click on the **Hide Wizard** button at the bottom of the screen to get rid of this.

The first thing to insert is the greeting. Use **WordArt** for this. Click on the

Figure 5.6 *The WordArt button*

button on the tools at the side, then create a place for this object on the page by putting the cross hairs at one corner, holding down the left mouse button and dragging to the other corner. (This need only be approximate as it can be altered later.) The screen will change and a new box will appear for the heading text stating, 'YOUR TEXT HERE'. Replace this with your text. To make the text form a particular shape, click on the drop-down arrow to the left of the toolbar and select one from the options shown. Other tools will allow you to change the font, specifying a particular size, adding shadows and lines, or changing the colour of it.

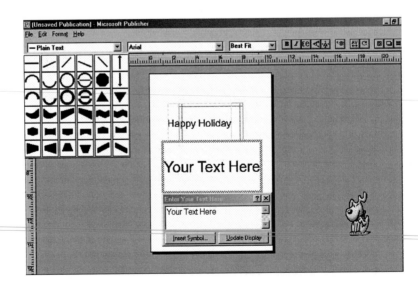

Figure 5.7 *The WordArt box with text shape options*

The drop-down menu shows you the options for shaping the title.

When you are happy with your title click **Update Display** or click outside of the box to return to the card.

The next step is to add an image. This time use the **Clip Art** tool.

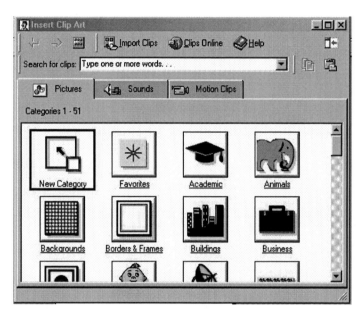

Figure 5.8 *The Clip Art button*

Again create a place for it then another dialog box will appear for you to choose the image.

Figure 5.9 *Select the clip art*

You can either do this by clicking on one of the categories and browsing, or by putting images to look for in the **Search for clips** box. If you are connected to the Internet, this might also include the images Microsoft provide on the Internet.

Once you find the image you want, click on it to select it. In the more recent versions of MS Publisher another box will appear.

Figure 5.10 *Inserting the clip art*

You will need to click on the top button, then close the dialog box by clicking on the X in the corner to get back to your publication. (Note: Sometimes the image you choose might not be available and a message will come up asking you to insert a CD or if you want the library cleaned up. This is because although a preview is available, not all the images have been copied in when the software was loaded. Clean up the gallery if you have time, otherwise just click **Cancel**.)

You will now have two objects on your page. To move either of them point at it and click to make it active and get the handles. As you move the cursor around the page you will notice it changes to a small lorry with 'Move' written on the side. If you point at a handle the cursor becomes a double-ended arrow pointing in the direction in which you can resize the object. If you work on a side, the image will change in one dimension only and can become distorted. If you point at a corner, both height and width will change simultaneously and therefore remain in proportion. Some objects also have another, usually green, dot above them: this is to allow you to rotate them.

You can place one object on top of the other if you wish, for instance a photo of a bunch of roses as a background and 'Be my valentine' over the top of it. To do this, simply move one object on top of the other then click on the **Arrange** menu and choose either **Send backward** or **Bring Forward** depending on what you want to happen.

Once you are happy with the front page, you can move to the greeting on the inside. Click on the number '3' at the bottom left of the page to move to the right place. For this section you can choose the **Text** tool.

Figure 5.11 *The text box tool*

Again draw the space for the text to go in. You will see the menus and toolbars change accordingly. When you begin to type your text it may be too small to see, in which case you can press the **F9** key at the top of the keyboard to zoom in, and again when you are finished to zoom out again.

As with a word processor, you can change the font, size and colour before you type or afterwards. Doing it last has advantages, as you can see how any changes will affect the layout, in which case you will need to highlight the text, either by dragging the cursor across all the text, by following **Edit>Select All** or by using the keyboard shortcut **Ctrl+A**. Whichever way you do it, once your text is highlighted you will be able to either use the toolbar or follow **Format>Font** to make the desired changes.

You will also be able to change the background colour and add a plain or patterned border to the box of any object. To change the background colour, simply click on the **Fill** tool (the slightly tipped bucket).

Figure 5.12 *The fill tool*

By clicking on the drop-down arrow you will have the option of selecting a colour from those shown, clicking on 'More Fill Colours' or choosing 'Fill Effects'. This last includes gradients, textures, patterns and pictures. It is worth playing with these to get a feel for the variety of backgrounds you can create. Gradients, for instance, are an effect of shading two colours together in different directions across the object.

To add a border to the object, either click on the **Line** tool or follow **Format>Line/Border/Style** then choose **More Styles.**

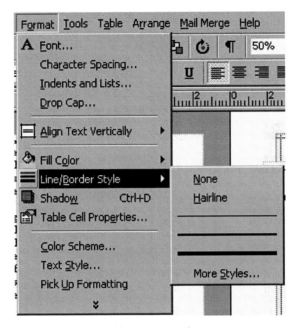

Figure 5.13 *Adding a border to an object*

This will offer a choice of styles and thicknesses, or you could click on the **Border Art** tab to get a range of effects including borders made up of images. There is also the option to change the colour and the thickness of the border.

Once you have written the message and changed the font style, size and colour, added a background and border, you are ready for the last stage.

Click on the number 4 on the bottom left and the back page will appear. Here you can add another text box showing that it is an original card, designed and printed by you (or the pupils).

Once you have printed it out you may want to make changes. Editing is straightforward. Double click on an object to make it active and change it. Once finished click away from it to get rid of the handles and move on to the next alteration.

When using MS Publisher you will find that every so often it prompts you to save your work. This is useful, particularly as these can be large files because of the number of graphics involved. If your computer is prone to running out of memory, it is as well to have the file saved.

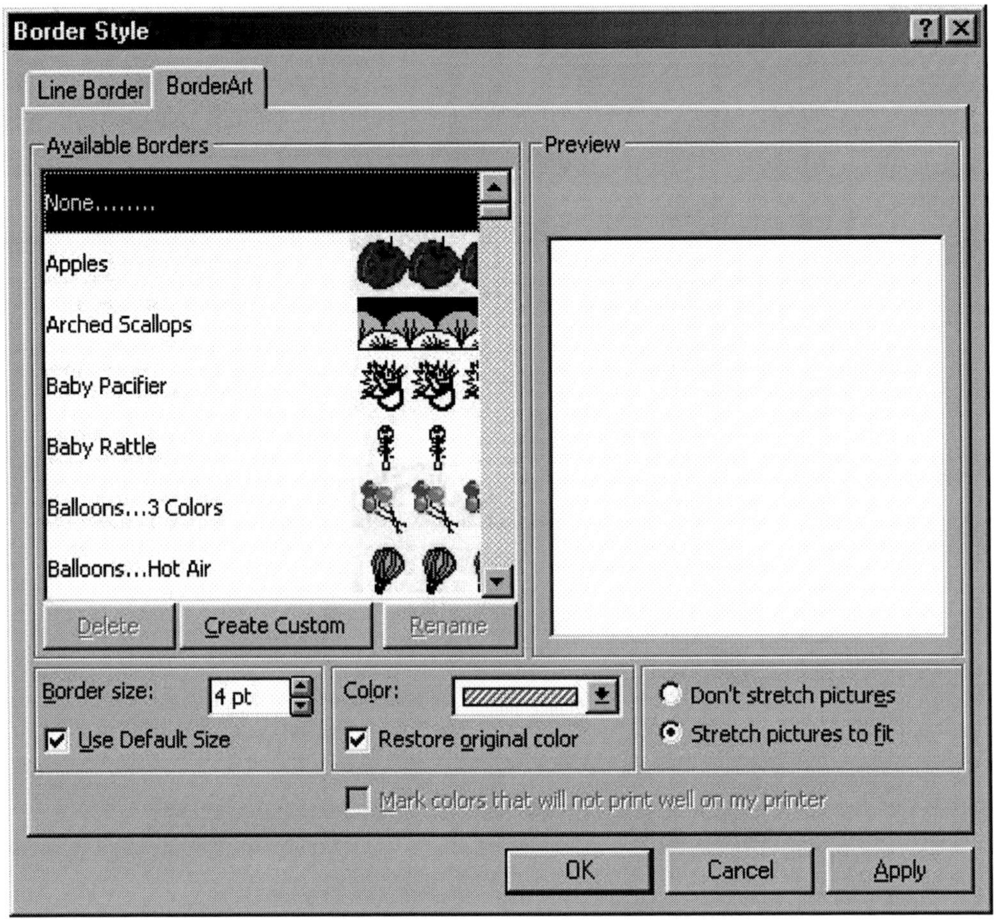

Figure 5.14 *Choosing border art*

Making a newsletter

Some activities may require you to insert information from a variety of sources. In making a class newspaper, children may have written stories with a word processor, drawn pictures with a paint program and taken photos or scanned them in. A useful exercise to practise these is to publish a newsletter about an alien.

Ask the pupils to write a newspaper report using a word processor as an interview with someone who has encountered an alien. They should also create a drawing of it from the description in the text using a graphics program such as 'Paint' or 'Colour Magic'. Also get them to take photos of people, yourself perhaps, to use as the witness.

To bring all of this together, start a new publication and choose the **Full page.** Add a title using **WordArt**, then use the **Insert** menu to bring in the other files. It is possible to bring them all together and place them around the edges of your page, on the grey area, dragging them in to place as you need them. MS Publisher will only print what is on the page – anything on the grey area, or even a fragment hanging off the edge, will not print.

Insert>Picture>From file will let you add both the drawing and the photo. You will need to know which folders they are in and click on the **Look in** box to go to these.

To add the text, first create a text box then choose **Insert>Text File** then find the file and click insert. One of the things that may happen is that the text is too big for the Text box. The program may ask if you want to use 'text flow'. This means that either another box will be created automatically or you can do it manually. If you choose the former, a small row of dots will appear at the bottom of it

Figure 5.15 *The text flow dots*

and another text box will appear to take the surplus. If you choose to do it manually, you will need to create a fresh text box: click on the **Text Link** tool

Figure 5.16 *The text link button*

and then on the first text box. Now when you click on the row of dots, the cursor will become an overflowing jug. Simply move this to the empty box and the text will be poured into it.

In this sort of layout you may want to move the graphics so that the text wraps around them or pulls in tight to them. To do this, choose **Format>Object** then choose **Wrapping**. This determines how the text and the graphics react to each other. 'Tight' will bring the text right around it; 'In line with text' will treat it as part of the text; and 'Square' will create a rectangular space in the text. Again experimenting with these will help you and the pupils to appreciate what they do. As always, if you do not like the change, simply click on the **Undo** button (or press **Ctrl+z**) to get rid of the change.

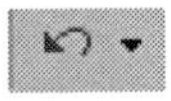

Figure 5.17 *The undo button*

The drop-down arrow lets you decide how many steps to reverse.

Once you have placed everything as you want it, print it out and read it through again. For some reason errors that are very easily seen on paper are often missed on screen.

Publishing packages for pupils

There are quite a lot of programs nowadays specifically designed for children. One example is '2Publish' from 2Simple Software which is designed for Key Stage 1 pupils. It offers a number of templates, such as four fold cards, wrapping paper and envelopes, and very easy-to-use tools. Graphics can be imported and elements such as the appearance of the font can be altered.

Another, more complex publisher is 'Textease 2000'. This is a powerful yet easy-to-use program. Different objects can be created and manipulated. It will write wherever you put the cursor. Sounds can also be added along with animations, so that publications can be on-screen as well as paper-based. This program comes as part of the Softease Studio suite, all of which work seamlessly together.

Desktop publishing lets you and the pupils create exciting, interesting publications which can be exploited regardless of the lesson. They could create a wanted poster for Goldilocks; an advert for a local history trail; a three-page flyer for or against fox-hunting. The format of the document can help give a context to the learning which makes it more realistic and therefore more effective.

CHAPTER 6

Using spreadsheets and databases

Although we mainly use our machines for creating written documents, their original purpose, as the name 'computer' suggests, was for calculating, for handling bits of data, for doing sums and sorting information much more quickly than we can do with pencil and paper. It is with spreadsheets and databases that we do this on modern desktops.

Essentially a spreadsheet is a large table made up of columns and rows into which we put the words and figures we want to work with, called 'data'. Data needs a context in order to give it meaning, for instance '26' might be a house number, the temperature outside, the number of people in a lottery syndicate or the goals conceded by Charlton Athletic at home last week. Spreadsheets can be used to perform calculations and to keep records. This latter use means making the spreadsheet work as a database, a way of sorting and ordering the information, in date or alphabetical order perhaps, in order to answer questions.

There are times when you will be harnessing the power of the spreadsheet to do both, to do calculations and to sort the answers. In your own work, you could calculate attendance percentages in a literacy group then put these in order, or keep a record of progress in learning key words and the rate at which these are being learnt. These figures could be compared to see if lack of progress is due to non-attendance or a deeper problem. With pupils you might gather weather information from around the world, then work out average temperatures and rainfall and compare places as holiday destinations.

The most widely used spreadsheet is Microsoft Excel. Here several pages, or worksheets, can be used simultaneously and information from one page can be used to do calculations or create charts and graphs on another. On a spreadsheet each column has a letter as a heading and each row a number. This means that each individual cell has its own address or reference such as A4 or FJ65. There can be up to 65,536 rows and 256 columns in each worksheet – a lot of data.

Using a spreadsheet for record keeping

Creating a table is very straightforward. Simply start a new worksheet then type the data into an empty cell, click in another one and add some more. To move quickly between cells either press the **Tab** key to move to the right or the **Return** or **Enter** key to move down. You will probably want to give your columns, and maybe your rows, titles or headings to describe the data. It is important not to leave blank rows because this prevents some tools from working fully.

This is an extract from a spreadsheet used as a database by a special educational needs co-ordinator (SENCO) to keep track of pupils with special educational needs in the school.

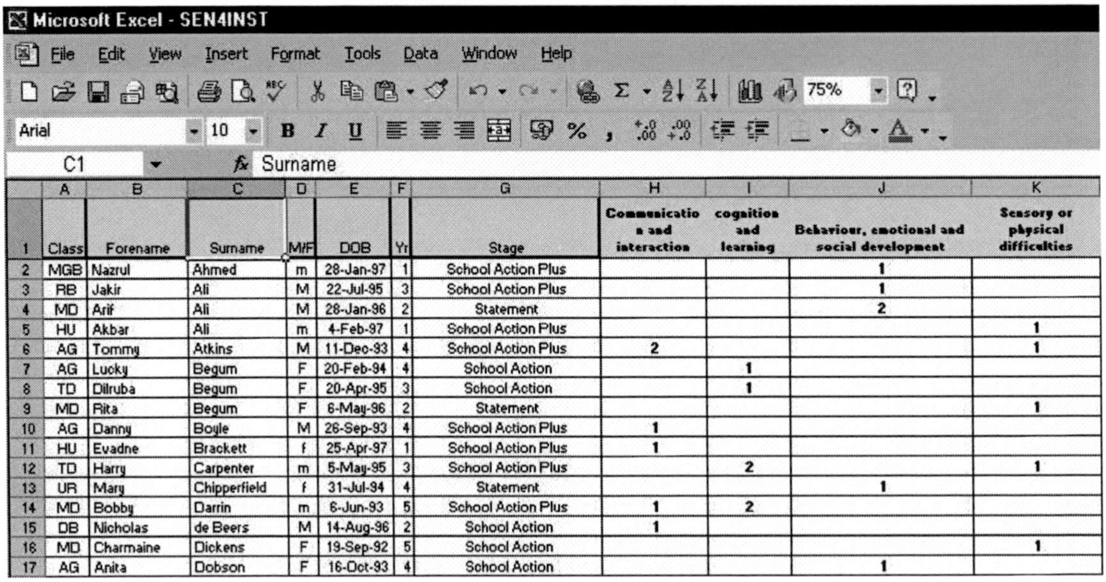

	Class	Forename	Surname	M/F	DOB	Yr	Stage	Communication and interaction	cognition and learning	Behaviour, emotional and social development	Sensory or physical difficulties
2	MGB	Nazrul	Ahmed	m	28-Jan-97	1	School Action Plus			1	
3	RB	Jakir	Ali	M	22-Jul-95	3	School Action Plus			1	
4	MD	Arif	Ali	M	28-Jan-96	2	Statement			2	
5	HU	Akbar	Ali	m	4-Feb-97	1	School Action Plus				1
6	AG	Tommy	Atkins	M	11-Dec-93	4	School Action Plus	2			1
7	AG	Lucky	Begum	F	20-Feb-94	4	School Action		1		
8	TD	Dilruba	Begum	F	20-Apr-95	3	School Action		1		
9	MD	Rita	Begum	F	6-May-96	2	Statement				1
10	AG	Danny	Boyle	M	26-Sep-93	4	School Action Plus	1			
11	HU	Evadne	Brackett	f	25-Apr-97	1	School Action Plus	1			
12	TD	Harry	Carpenter	m	5-May-95	3	School Action Plus		2		1
13	UR	Mary	Chipperfield	f	31-Jul-94	4	Statement			1	
14	MD	Bobby	Darrin	m	6-Jun-93	5	School Action Plus	1	2		
15	DB	Nicholas	de Beers	M	14-Aug-96	2	School Action	1			
16	MD	Charmaine	Dickens	F	19-Sep-92	5	School Action				1
17	AG	Anita	Dobson	F	16-Oct-93	4	School Action			1	

Figure 6.1 *Extract from a typical SEN register*

The **Column Headings** are coloured yellow to make them stand out. The data includes what SEN stage (School Action, School Action Plus or Statement) the pupils are at and which of four categories represents their primary and, in some cases, secondary needs. Currently the information is in alphabetical order. The **Sort** facility can be used to change this to date of birth (DOB in the example). To do this you would follow **Data>Sort** and this dialog box will open.

Figure 6.2 *Sort dialog box*

The **Header row** box needs to be checked for the spreadsheet to use the titles for the sort, otherwise the titles will be used as data and end up somewhere else on the sheet.

Following this **sort** the data looks like this.

	A	B	C	D	E	F	G	H	I	J	K
	Class	Forename	Surname	M/F	DOB	Yr	Stage	Communication and interaction	cognition and learning	Behaviour, emotional and social development	Sensory or physical difficulties
2	EB	Oliver	Stanley	m	3-Oct-91	6	School Action Plus	1			
3	EB	Lee	Rogers	m	27-Nov-91	6	School Action Plus		1	2	
4	EB	Terry	Marsh	M	29-May-92	6	School Action Plus			1	
5	MD	Charmaine	Dickens	F	19-Sep-92	5	School Action				1
6	MD	Bobby	Darrin	m	6-Jun-93	5	School Action Plus	1	2		
7	MD	James	Hunt	m	23-Jun-93	5	School Action			1	
8	AG	Danny	Boyle	M	26-Sep-93	4	School Action Plus	1			
9	AG	Anita	Dobson	F	16-Oct-93	4	School Action			1	
10	AG	Doris	Withers	F	2-Nov-93	4	School Action		1	2	
11	AG	Tommy	Atkins	M	11-Dec-93	4	School Action Plus	2			1
12	AG	John	Ford	M	31-Jan-94	4	School Action	1			
13	AG	Lucky	Begum	F	20-Feb-94	4	School Action		1		
14	AG	Ho	Luk	F	25-Feb-94	4	School Action			1	
15	UR	Hassan	Miah	M	23-Jul-94	4	School Action		1		
16	UR	Mary	Chipperfield	f	31-Jul-94	4	Statement			1	
17	UR	Hassina	Nessa	F	26-Aug-94	4	School Action			1	
18	TD	Dean	Murphy	M	15-Dec-94	3	School Action Plus	1			
19	TD	Dilruba	Begum	F	20-Apr-95	3	School Action		1		
20	TD	Harry	Carpenter	m	5-May-95	3	School Action Plus		2		1
21	TD	Warren	Mitchell	M	31-May-95	3	Statement			1	
22	RB	Matthew	Kelly	M	11-Jun-95	3	School Action	1			
23	RB	Jakir	Ali	M	22-Jul-95	3	School Action Plus			1	

Figure 6.3 *SEN register in date of birth order*

The oldest children come first because the data is in **Ascending** order.

Another similar facility of a spreadsheet is the **Filter**. This allows us to choose which **Records** (individual sets of data) we want to see. For instance, I may only want to see pupils with Statements;

	A	B	C	D	E	F	G	H	I	J	K
1	Cl.	Forename	Surname		DOE		Stage	Communication and interaction	cognition and learning	Behaviour, emotional and social development	Sensory or physical difficulties
16	UR	Mary	Chipperfield	f	31-Jul-94	4	Statement			1	
21	TD	Warren	Mitchell	M	31-May-95	3	Statement	1			
24	RB	Shobell	Miah	M	5-Aug-95	3	Statement			1	
27	MD	Arif	Ali	M	28-Jan-96	2	Statement	1		2	
28	MD	Rita	Begum	F	6-May-96	2	Statement	1			

Figure 6.4 *Pupils with Statements*

or just the girls;

	A	B	C	D	E	F	G	H	I	J	K
1	Cl.	Forename	Surname		DOE		Stage	Communication and interaction	cognition and learning	Behaviour, emotional and social development	Sensory or physical difficulties
5	MD	Charmaine	Dickens	F	19-Sep-92	5	School Action				1
9	AG	Anita	Dobson	F	16-Oct-93	4	School Action			1	
10	AG	Doris	Withers	F	2-Nov-93	4	School Action		1	2	
13	AG	Lucky	Begum	F	20-Feb-94	4	School Action		1		
14	AG	Ho	Luk	F	25-Feb-94	4	School Action			1	
16	UR	Mary	Chipperfield	f	31-Jul-94	4	Statement			1	
17	UR	Hassina	Nessa	F	26-Aug-94	4	School Action			1	
19	TD	Dilruba	Begum	F	20-Apr-95	3	School Action		1		
28	MD	Rita	Begum	F	6-May-96	2	Statement	1			
35	HU	Evadne	Brackett	f	25-Apr-97	1	School Action Plus	1			

Figure 6.5 *Filtered for girls*

or only those with communication and interaction difficulties;

	A	B	C	D	E	F	G	H Communicatio n and interactio	I cognition and learnin	J Behaviour, emotional and social development	K Sensory or physical difficulties
1	Cl.	Forenam	Surname	N	DOE		Stage				
2	EB	Oliver	Stanley	m	3-Oct-91	6	School Action Plus	1			
6	MD	Bobby	Darrin	m	6-Jun-93	5	School Action Plus	1	2		
8	AG	Danny	Boyle	M	26-Sep-93	4	School Action Plus	1			
11	AG	Tommy	Atkins	M	11-Dec-93	4	School Action Plus	2			1
12	AG	John	Ford	M	31-Jan-94	4	School Action	1			
18	TD	Dean	Murphy	M	15-Dec-94	3	School Action Plus	1			
21	TD	Warren	Mitchell	M	31-May-95	3	Statement	1			
22	RB	Matthew	Kelly	M	11-Jun-95	3	School Action	1			
26	MD	Gbenga	Ikoli	M	15-Sep-95	2	School Action	2	1		
27	MD	Arif	Ali	M	28-Jan-96	2	Statement	1		2	
28	MD	Rita	Begum	F	6-May-96	2	Statement	1			
29	DB	Christopher	Isherway	M	1-Jul-96	2	School Action Plus	1			
31	DB	Nicholas	de Beers	M	14-Aug-96	2	School Action	1			
35	HU	Evadne	Brackett	f	25-Apr-97	1	School Action Plus	1			

Figure 6.6 *Filtered for communication difficulties*

or even only those children who meet all of these criteria.

	A	B	C	D	E	F	G	H Communicatio n and interactio	I cognition and learnin	J Behaviour, emotional and social development	K Sensory or physical difficulties
1	Cl.	Forenam	Surname	N	DOE		Stage				
28	MD	Rita	Begum	F	6-May-96	2	Statement	1			
36											
37											
38											

Figure 6.7 *Filtered for all of the above*

The **Filter** function lets you narrow the records down to see only those that meet specific criteria. To use this you place the cursor in the headings row by simply clicking on one of the 'Row headers', then follow **Data>Filter>Autofilter.** A small arrow will appear in the corner of each heading as in the illustrations above. When you click on one of these it will show all the different entries in that column plus a couple of other options, such as 'blanks' or 'non-blanks'. You simply select the entry to sort by and click on it. So to get a list of the pupils in any particular class, you click on the arrow and select the class from this list.

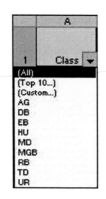

Figure 6.8 *List for filtering by class*

To stop filtering by that criterion, simply click on 'All'. The 'Custom' function allows you to use 'and' and 'or' to filter by more than one entry, or to do more complex actions such as finding results that are 'greater than' or 'less than' or that have a particular beginning or ending.

Databases in the curriculum

The **Sort** and **Filter** functions allow us to interrogate data, to ask questions of it. Spreadsheets such as Excel are just one of the tools used to handle data in lessons. Other programs are specifically designed for the purpose and therefore can be easier to use as they offer more support to the user. Essentially, though, they are doing the same thing, allowing users to ask questions of data.

This spreadsheet on pets can be interrogated by skin type, classification or number of legs.

	A	B	C	D	E
1	Animal	Name	Skin covering	Number of legs	Classification
2	Rat	Ratty	Fur	4	Mammal
3	Rabbit	Floppy	Fur	4	Mammal
4	Parrot	Mr. Big	Feathers	2	Bird
5	Guinea Pig	Snuffles	Fur	4	Mammal
6	Goldfish	Eric	Scales	0	Fish
7	Horse	Goldie	Fur	4	Mammal
8	Snake	Sid	Skin	0	Reptile
9	Budgerigar	Squeak	Feathers	2	Bird
10	Dog	Bruno	Fur	4	Mammal
11	Cat	Tibbles	Fur	4	Mammal
12	Cat	Nelson	Fur	4	Mammal
13	Mouse	Speedy	Fur	4	Mammal

Figure 6.9 *Pets spreadsheet*

With a database designed for school children, you might get a search screen like this that uses a number of questions to perform the filtering function.

Here you can see the term, 'Is it a mammal is the same as Yes' has already been selected and the 'Or number of legs is the same as 4' is being added. This will show all mammals and any other animals that have four legs.

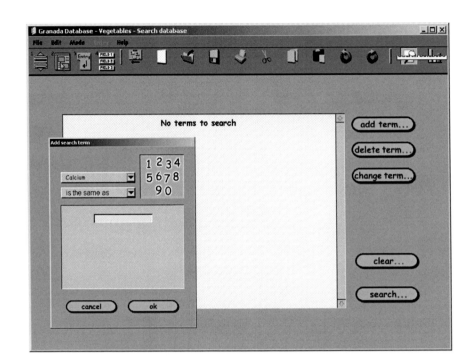

Figure 6.10 *Search screen from Granada Toolkit database*

Creating a graph

All data handling programs will create charts and graphs from the information you provide. In Excel this is done by highlighting the cells to be included then clicking on the **Chart Wizard** button.

Figure 6.11 *Chart wizard button*

You can select cells that are not adjacent by holding down the **Control key** while selecting.

To create a bar chart showing how many legs each animal has, you would start by highlighting the 'Animal' and the 'Number of legs' columns.

	A	B	C	D	E
1	Animal	Name	Skin covering	Number of legs	Classification
2	Rat	Ratty	Fur	4	Mammal
3	Rabbit	Floppy	Fur	4	Mammal
4	Parrot	Mr. Big	Feathers	2	Bird
5	Guinea Pig	Snuffles	Fur	4	Mammal
6	Goldfish	Eric	Scales	0	Fish
7	Horse	Goldie	Fur	4	Mammal
8	Snake	Sid	Skin	0	Reptile
9	Budgerigar	Squeak	Feathers	2	Bird
10	Dog	Bruno	Fur	4	Mammal
11	Cat	Tibbles	Fur	4	Mammal
12	Cat	Nelson	Fur	4	Mammal
13	Mouse	Speedy	Fur	4	Mammal

Figure 6.12 *Highlighting non-adjacent columns*

Clicking on the **Chart Wizard** button allows you to choose the type of chart required.

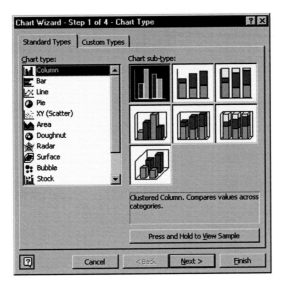

Figure 6.13 *Chart Wizard choices*

To complete the chart, click **Next** adding labels and a title as you go. When you click **Finish**, your chart will appear.

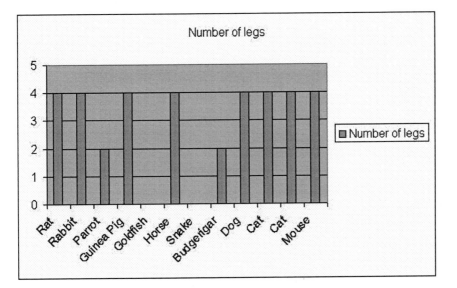

Figure 6.14 *Completed bar chart*

Using a spreadsheet to do calculations

One of the most useful functions of a spreadsheet is to instantly do calculations and recalculate much faster than can be done using pencil and paper or a calculator. When using a spreadsheet to do calculations, there are a couple of things it is important to remember: firstly that formulas always start with an equals sign '='; secondly that while plus and minus remain '+' and '−', divide becomes '/' and times '*'.

A typical activity with pupils (or even for your own purposes) is to use the spreadsheet to calculate the cost of holding a party. In this example there are a restricted number of food and drink items and the prices are given, as below.

	A	B	C	D
1	Item	Number of items	Cost per item	Cost
2	crisps (pack of 6)		1.15	
3	cakes (pack of six)		1.25	
4	Samosas (meat)		1.75	
5	Samosas (veg)		1.75	
6	Pizzas (each)		1.99	
7	Jaffa cakes (packet)		0.81	
8	Cheese balls (packet)		0.45	
9	KitKat (pack of 4)		1.19	
10	Cola (1.5 litres)		1.45	
11	Lemonade (1.5 litres)		0.99	
12			Total Cost	
13			Money collected	
14			Left to spend	

Figure 6.15 *Calculating the costs of a party*

The cost currently does not have a pound sign, but we can add this automatically. First of all the whole column is highlighted by clicking on its letter, C in this case, then choosing **Format>Cells**, selecting Currency and choosing two decimal places.

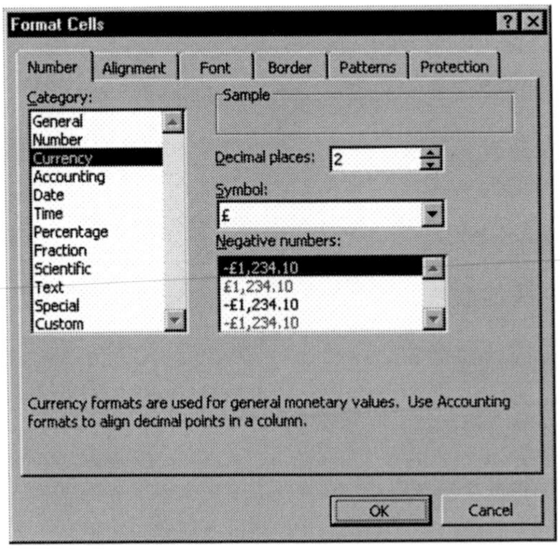

Figure 6.16 *Formatting cells as currency*

Now when data is entered it will automatically be set out as pounds and pence. The same formatting can be applied to row D.

You can see from the list the various types of data **format** that can be used. This can help make sure that particular columns conform to particular types of data, such as **dates** or **percentages**. However, any entry that mixes letters and numbers, post codes for instance, can only have **Text** format.

To calculate the amount spent on each item we will multiply the 'Number of items' by the cost per item, so if we wanted six multipacks of crisps we would times 6 by £1.15. The point of using a spreadsheet is that it lets us try different numbers and will, if we set it up properly, recalculate automatically each time. When we use a formula, we can tell the computer to multiply the contents of one cell by the contents of another, in this case cell B2 (the number of packets of crisps) by cell C2 (the price per packet). If either number is changed, the 'Cost' column will change automatically. The formula in cell D2 will be =B2*C2. And the one in D3 will be =B3*C3 and so on down.

	A	B	C	D
1	Item	Number of items	Cost per item	Cost
2	crisps (pack of 6)		1.15	=B2*C2
3	cakes (pack of six)		1.25	=B3*C3
4	Samosas (meat)		1.75	=B4*C4
5	Samosas (veg)		1.75	=B5*C5
6	Pizzas (each)		1.99	=B6*C6
7	Jaffa cakes (packet)		0.81	=B7*C7
8	Cheese balls (packet)		0.45	=B8*C8
9	KitKat (pack of 4)		1.19	=B9*C9
10	Cola (1.5 litres)		1.45	=B10*C10
11	Lemonade (1.5 litres)		0.99	=B11*C11
12			Total Cost	
13			Money collected	
14			Left to spend	

Figure 6.17 *Party with item costs filled in*

(Note: to copy the formulas quickly we can type in the first one then pick up the small black handle on the corner of the cell and pull it down over the rest of the cells beneath.)

Now when we start our shopping list, the amount we are spending will be automatically filled in like this.

	A	B	C	D
1	Item	Number of items	Cost per item	Cost
2	crisps (pack of 6)	6	£1.15	£6.90
3	cakes (pack of six)	6	£1.25	£7.50
4	Samosas (meat)	4	£1.75	£7.00
5	Samosas (veg)	4	£1.75	£7.00
6	Pizzas (each)	4	£1.99	£7.96
7	Jaffa cakes (packet)	2	£0.81	£1.62
8	Cheese balls (packet)	2	£0.45	£0.90
9	KitKat (pack of 4)	6	£1.19	£7.14
10	Cola (1.5 litres)	3	£1.45	£4.35
11	Lemonade (1.5 litres)	3	£0.99	£2.97
12			Total Cost	
13			Money collected	
14			Left to spend	

Figure 6.18 *Party with total costs filled in*

Finally we need to know how much the 'Total Cost' is and take it away from the money collected to see how much we have left to spend. We want to know the **SUM** spent. Again we are not going to put in each individual amount, (=£6.90+£7.50+£7.00 and so on), we are going to tell the computer which cells to add up. It would be laborious if we had to put in each one, so we just use the range of cells by specifying the first one and the last one with a colon in between and put this in brackets. In this case that is (D2:D11). As always the formula begins with an ' = ' sign, and we are using the sum function, so it comes out as '=SUM(D2:D11)'. If you get any part of it wrong the computer will flag it up with '#Value' or '#NAME?' to let you know.

If we assume there are 30 children in the class, each bringing in £2.00 for the party, this will give us £60 'Money collected'. The amount 'Left to spend' will then be =60–D12, because this value is not going to change. The formulas in your final spreadsheet will look like this.

	A	B	C	D
1	Item	Number of items	Cost per item	Cost
2	crisps (pack of 6)	6	1.15	=B2*C2
3	cakes (pack of six)	6	1.25	=B3*C3
4	Samosas (meat)	4	1.75	=B4*C4
5	Samosas (veg)	4	1.75	=B5*C5
6	Pizzas (each)	4	1.99	=B6*C6
7	Jaffa cakes (packet)	2	0.81	=B7*C7
8	Cheese balls (packet)	2	0.45	=B8*C8
9	KitKat (pack of 4)	6	1.19	=B9*C9
10	Cola (1.5 litres)	3	1.45	=B10*C10
11	Lemonade (1.5 litres)	3	0.99	=B11*C11
12			Total Cost	=SUM(D2:D11)
13			Money collected	60
14			Left to spend	=D13-D12

Figure 6.19 *Final layout for party*

When used in this way, a spreadsheet can be thought of as a 'Model', that is a representation of a real situation that we can use to ask 'What if?' questions. 'What if we get another packet of samosas?' or 'What if the price of pizzas goes up, how many can we afford then?' The idea in this simulation is to spend all the money. It is important for the adults working with the children to help them to focus on the real situation. They could buy 20 pizzas and 20 bottles of lemonade, but would that satisfy everyone present? You can also extend the idea by adding in entertainment or cutting down the number of people attending. The challenge is to create a realistic party for the budget available.

Spreadsheets are a very powerful data-handling tool which users can get to grips with quickly, sorting information or performing calculations. They can also be used in more complex ways such as providing the data for a mail merge or modelling changes in environmental factors in a greenhouse. When you are creating one, it saves time and effort if you know how you want to use it, the questions you want answered, before you begin. That way you will know what information to collect, how to lay it out and what formulas you will need to put into it.

CHAPTER 7

Using presentation programs

Computers make it possible to quickly and easily put together presentations that combine images, text, sound and video – what we know as 'multimedia authoring'. You will be familiar with the results from the ubiquitous use of PowerPoint for presentations: text will fly in from all angles accompanied by sound effects and lists of bullet points will drop into place to emphasise a point the speaker is making. While such programs were designed for this purpose, they can be used to quickly and easily create other sorts of resources, such as books and websites. Pupils will be familiar with these kinds of resources from their use of CD-ROMs and the Internet.

It is well worth getting to know Microsoft PowerPoint, the most widely used of the presentation programs, for a number of reasons. Firstly, it is probable that in the not very distant future all classrooms will have interactive whiteboards from which whole-class teaching will be done. Teaching assistants may find that one of the ways they will be supporting classes is by creating resources to use on the whiteboard. PowerPoint is one of the quickest and easiest ways to make these.

Secondly, pupils will increasingly be using multimedia authoring as part of their learning; where once they wrote essays, soon they will be creating presentations as a means of expressing themselves. Some pupils will find this liberating as they can use other means, such as sound and images, to get their message across. Currently creating presentations tends to begin in the last years of primary school, although even infants can do it with a bit of support.

Thirdly, it can be used to create off-screen resources such as books and leaflets quickly and easily, in some cases more readily than with purpose-built software such as MS Publisher. The chart facility will instantly create a graph more simply than Excel.

As with all programs, there are a number of ways of performing the same task and you will learn the ones that suit you best. However, as you will see, with PowerPoint most of what you will want to do can be found under the **Insert** menu.

Creating presentations

You may find that you are creating presentations as part of a curriculum project with pupils, as a tool for teaching or to inform parents at a parents' evening about a proposed school journey. In whichever case, the process is the same.

Quite often children are taught particular ICT skills in ICT lessons which they then put into practice across the curriculum, so while they might do a presentation about themselves in ICT, they may apply it in science. The presentation used for illustration here is about 'Space'.

In a class activity, different pupils or groups of pupils could be allocated specific topics such as 'The Planets' or 'Living in Space'. These can be linked together using **hyperlinks** as you will see later.

When you first start PowerPoint, it may do one of two things depending on which version of the program you have. Either it will start directly with a new presentation, or it will ask if you want to start a new presentation or open an existing one, in which case you will need to choose the former to get a first slide on screen. Whenever you start a new presentation it will offer you a title slide, like this.

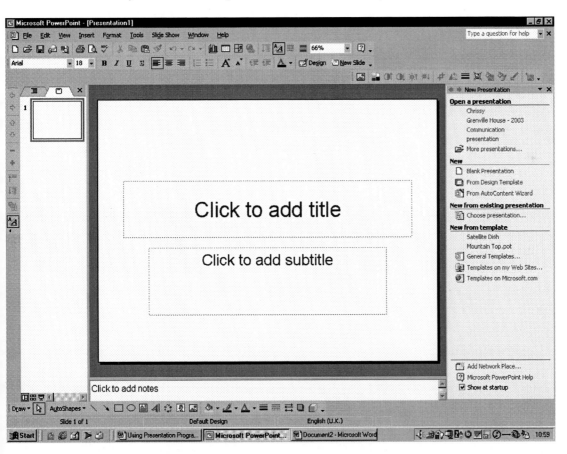

Figure 7.1 *The title slide in PowerPoint comes up automatically*

This page is a 'template'. PowerPoint has many of these to support the creative process. On the left you can choose to see thumbnails of your slides, or an outline of the points added so far. As you can see, you can simply click on a box and type to begin. Here we can type 'Space' and 'by John Galloway'.

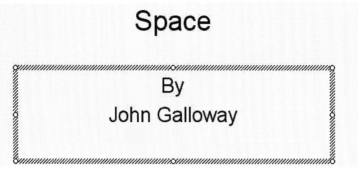

Figure 7.2 *Space title slide*

We can also add colour and animations. These can be on individual objects, the graphics and text boxes you create, or to the whole slide.

As mentioned, when creating a presentation, most things can be done from the **Insert** menu. To add a second slide follow **Insert>New Slide.** At this point the available templates will appear, either as a new dialog box on screen or as a sidebar. These have predetermined spaces for bullet points, graphics, graphs and even sound and video clips. This is a selection of those available in PowerPoint 2002.

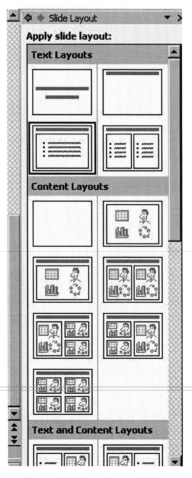

Figure 7.3 *Templates sidebar*

If you choose the blank slide you can add whatever you want, again working through the **Insert** menu.

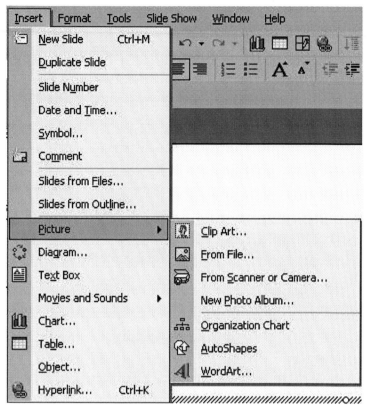

Figure 7.4 *Insert menu*

From this illustration you can see that when you choose to add a **Picture** you have the options to use:

● 'Clip art', which is graphics that come with the program;

● 'From File', which is graphics that you have created and saved somewhere, such as photos or drawings;

● 'From Scanner or Camera', which will connect directly to whichever of these is connected to the computer;

● 'New Photo Album', which lets you quickly make an on-screen album;

● 'Organization Chart', which lets you create a diagram of several levels;

● 'Autoshapes', which are such things as stars and speech bubbles;

● and 'WordArt', which gives you headings in shaped formats.

The first slide of my presentation will be about 'The Planets' and to add impact it will use 'WordArt' for a title. Choosing this from the **Picture** sub-menu brings up this dialog box. (Note: WordArt may vary according to the program you are using, as with Publisher 2000 in Chapter 5.)

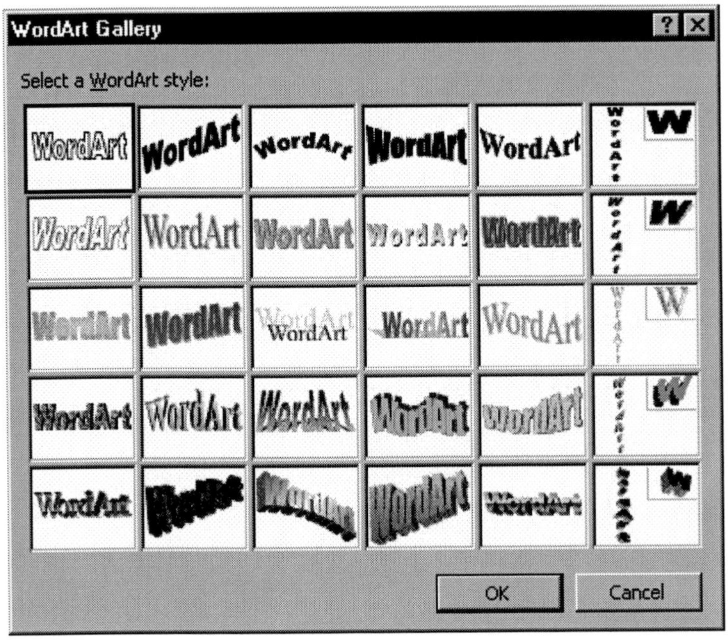

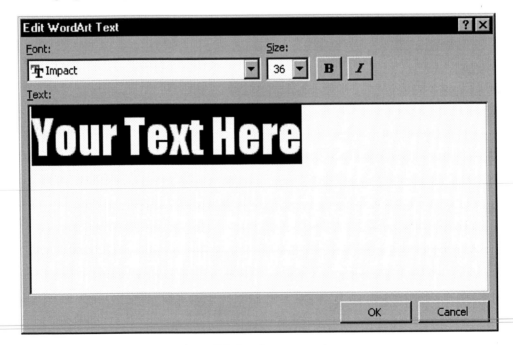

Figure 7.5 *WordArt menu*

You select the style of title, and then this box where you type in the caption. When you click **OK** a separate tool bar will appear with which you can reformat it, changing font style and colour, add a shadow and so on.

Figure 7.6 *Entering your caption*

Figure 7.7 *The WordArt toolbar*

To add an image to illustrate the subject, open the **Picture** sub-menu and choose the source, in this case **Clip Art**. What appears will again depend on your version of PowerPoint. In the 2002 sidebar you will type a search term into the 'Search text' box.

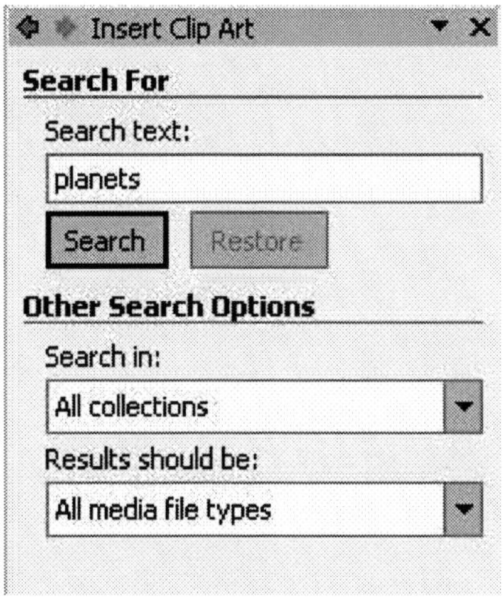

Figure 7.8 *Clip art sidebar*

The additional options, 'Search in' and 'Results should be', will broaden or restrict the search.

A search for 'Planets' may find more than 40 images, any of which can be easily inserted. (Sometimes clip art will preview images that it does not have in its library, which can be frustrating. It might be as well to run the tidying tool it offers at such times to get rid of these.) It is also possible to use images from the Internet – the **Clips Online** option will automatically search the Microsoft site or a clip could be copied following a search (see Chapter 10 Using the Internet). When using an image from the Internet, it is important to observe any copyright restrictions, and to acknowledge the source, particularly if you are going to publish the document as a book or website. (See Chapter 17 Legal knowledge for more on copyright.)

Once inserted the 'object' can be moved, resized using the 'handles' on the edges, or rotated. If the handles (small white dots) are not visible, click on the object once.

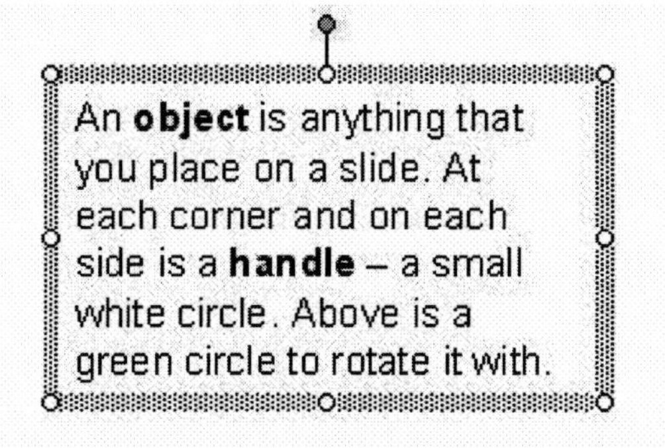

An **object** is anything that you place on a slide. At each corner and on each side is a **handle** – a small white circle. Above is a green circle to rotate it with.

Figure 7.9 *Example of an object*

As you move the cursor over the object, it will change shape as different options become available.

The normal cursor (Figure 7.10), will change to the 'move' cursor, shown in Figure 7.11, the 'resize' cursor, available when over a 'handle' as in Figure 7.12, and the **rotate** cursor, shown in Figure 7.13.

Figure 7.10 *Select arrow*

Figure 7.11 *Move cursor*

Figure 7.12 *Resize cursor*

Figure 7.13 *Rotate cursor*

To add writing a **text box** can be added, again from the **Insert** menu. The text can be formatted just as in a word processor.

You can also change the colour scheme of the slide in the **Format** menu, either using a **Slide design** which offers lots of different professional-looking layouts, or by using **Background** which just changes the colour of either one slide or all of them. This can transform the presentation instantly into something more interesting.

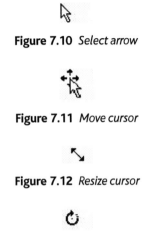

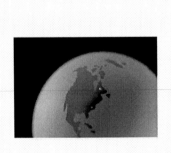

There are nine planets circling the sun. Earth is the third nearest.

Figure 7.14 *PowerPoint slide with an unformatted background*

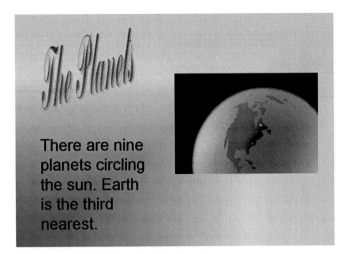

Figure 7.15 *Slide with gradient fill effect applied*

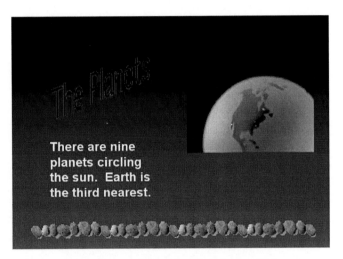

Figure 7.16 *Slide with rock design applied*

When all the slides have been completed the presentation can be viewed through one of three routes: by following **Slide Show>View Show**; by pressing **F5** on the keyboard; or by clicking on the View Show button on the **Slide View toolbar**. This can be found at the bottom left of the screen.

Figure 7.17 *Slide view options*

The other views available include **Normal**, which shows the layout of the slide and the contents in sidebar to the left (as in Figure 7.1 above), and **Slide Sorter**, which shows them as a storyboard so that you can move them around to change the order.

When viewing a show, slides are advanced by clicking the mouse button, the space bar, the enter key or by using the navigation arrows on the keyboard. This is like turning the pages of a book. However, another way of moving between slides, in a non-linear manner, is to use **hyperlinks**. These work like links on the Internet, where you click on a word, sentence or object and jump to another place. In the Space presentation it could be:

- to a list of the planets

- from the name of a planet to a slide with particular information about it

- to a website

Hyperlinks can again be accessed through the **Insert** menu, following **Insert>Hyperlink.** First of all, the object or text to be linked needs to be highlighted. With text this is done in the usual way by holding down the mouse button and running the cursor over it. With an object this is done by clicking to make it active, that is with its 'handles' showing. (With a text box you need to click on the edge of the box itself to get the 'close-grained' edge.) The **hyperlink** menu looks like this.

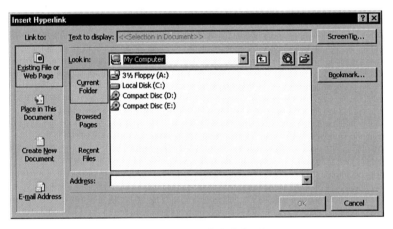

Figure 7.18 *Hyperlink dialog box*

There are a number of options for links. One is to any document on the computer, another is to a website by entering an address. You can also create links between slides. To link the word 'Planets' from the second slide to a list of them would be to a **Place in This Document**.

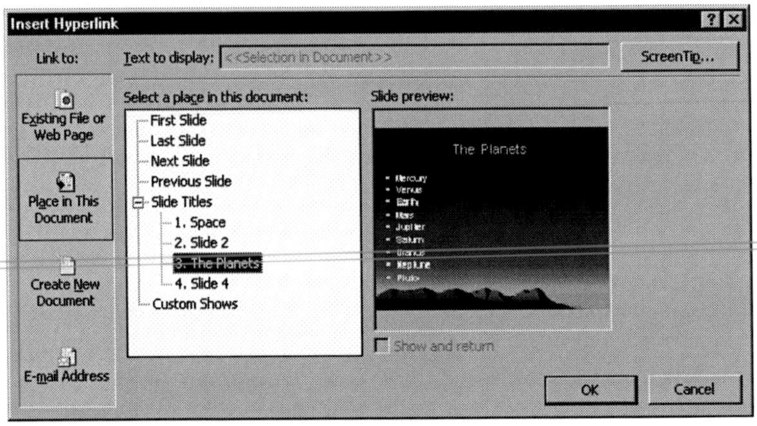

Figure 7.19 *Hyperlink to another slide*

A preview is shown of the available slides. The hyperlink is created by simply selecting the slide to link to and clicking **OK**.

When using **hyperlinks** it may be necessary to switch off the automatic page turning, which can be done by following **Slide Show>Hide Slide**. Now slides are not automatically opened at the click of a mouse or key but when linked to.

When a hyperlink is present on a slide, the cursor will change to the **browser finger** when it passes over it. Any text links will be underlined and, like on a web page, may change colour once they have been followed.

Figure 7.20 *The browser finger*

This interactivity means that PowerPoint can be used to create websites. Simply follow **File>Save as Web Page** and it will automatically format the pages and their content for use on a website. This will also allow the presentation to be viewed in web-browsing software such as **Internet Explorer**. Apart from posting on the Internet this option can also allow pupils to take copies home to view when they do not have PowerPoint on their own machines. However, another option is to use **Pack and Go**, also in the **File** menu, as this adds a 'viewer' to the presentation so it can be used on any machine.

Presentations can also be printed out and used as books. By selecting **Handouts**, the number of slides per page can be set at anything from one to nine. Choosing two to a page makes an A5 booklet; using four or more can give a comic strip effect. This could be used with clip art or photos and speech bubbles to create books such as stories or collections of jokes.

Figure 7.21 *Using graphics and speech bubbles*

Adding speech bubbles

To add speech bubbles to a slide, follow **Insert>Picture>AutoShapes** then choose the speech bubbles from the **AutoShapes** toolbar. These can be altered as with any object. Text is inserted by simply typing when the object is active, and the background colour can be changed by using the fill bucket on the drawing toolbar (as discussed in Chapter 5 on using desktop publishing). This is usually visible on the bottom of the screen; if not, bring it up by following **View>Toolbars>Drawing**.

Adding sounds

It is also quite straightforward to add sounds. These can be from the available library or easily recorded. To do this follow **Insert>Movies and Sounds>** then choose one of the options. If you choose **Record Sound** you can record your voice and make a talking book. The text could be read as you open the page, or by clicking on the speaker icon that appears.

You can even attach the sound to an object so that it is activated by clicking on it. This is one of the **Action Settings** to be found in the **Slide Show** menu. Here you will also find **Animation Schemes**, which determine how an object enters the presentation, and **Slide Transition**, which is how one slide changes to the next.

Other options, such as **Rehearse Timings**, automatically move the presentation on after a given time. This is useful if you are going to have it running for people to view, perhaps playing a looping introduction to the school in the reception area.

With a few relatively simple techniques you can create quite sophisticated resources, combining text, images and even sounds to good effect. Hyperlinks will let you create tools such as quizzes to use in class, or adventure stories where the reader chooses which path to follow. The use of speech bubbles and pupils' own voices can create books where they literally read to themselves, and the printing options mean your creations can be appreciated away from the computer as well as on it.

CHAPTER 8

Using a control program

Putting a cardboard box on your head then asking children to direct you around the room is often the first step in teaching children how to program computers. There are admittedly a great number of steps from there until they begin creating the games they all want to make, but everyone has to start somewhere.

From demonstrating the process of controlling a machine through risking your knees on low-level chairs by blindly stumbling around the room, the next step is usually the use of a 'floor turtle' such as a 'Pixie' or a 'Roamer'.

Figure 8.1a *Floor turtle*

Figure 8.1b *Roamer*

Floor turtle

You will have emphasised to the children the need to be clear and precise in their instructions and the sequencing of them. The first exercise, where you are the turtle, gives opportunities for lots of teaching points and will allow you to make it clear just what commands will bring about what result. When moving on to the actual floor turtle, the pupils will input their list of instructions then press 'go' and watch it wander off. While there are mats available with streets and buildings on them to provide a context for the exercise, you can just as easily set up a maze on the floor with masking tape and challenge the pupils to program the machine to get through it.

Some pupils may find it difficult to make the conceptual leap from the programmable robot on the floor to the arrow moving around the screen, which is the next step in the process. Remote control cars that can be programmed from the computer are available and it might be worth suggesting your school buys one.

Moving onto the screen

Once you do get on the screen, you will be using a program based on 'Logo'. This was first developed by Seymore Papert in the 1970s as a teaching tool. By programming an on-screen turtle, he believed that pupils could be offered challenges and problems, the solutions to which would bring about learning. There are now several of these types of programs on the market, and the original version can be found and downloaded freely from the Internet.

The original program relies entirely on commands, whereas nowadays programs use buttons to choose direction, turns and distance.

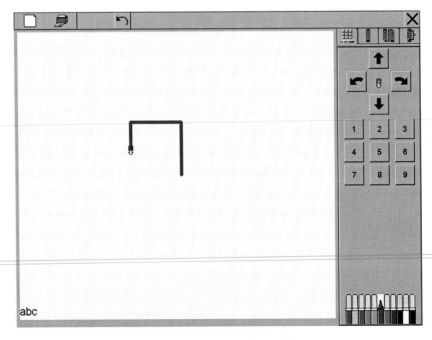

Figure 8.2 *Using 2Go with arrow keys.*

This screenshot from '2Go' from 2Simple Software gives arrows for forward and backwards, turn left and turn right. Like similar programs, it can be easily altered to give arrows for diagonals, to remove the need for distance and to follow a flow diagram. Different backgrounds can also be used to provide different challenges.

Here the car has been programmed to travel from the red house to the green one. The steps can be watched as the program runs and quickly edited.

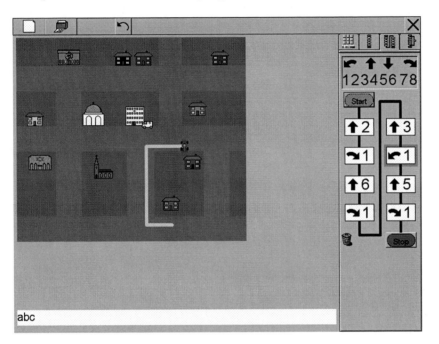

Figure 8.3 *Using a flowchart to sequence actions.*

These programs lend themselves to setting different challenges for pupils of different abilities. While you might ask one child to draw a square, you might ask another to draw a series of squares of different sizes one inside the other. The backgrounds will let them guide the turtle from one place to another and they can move on to more difficult geometric shapes, such as hexagons, or to teach the computer to write their initials.

While this is still a long way from learning the code to create their own 'shoot em ups' (fast-action, arcade-style games), they will have learnt the basic process of sequencing instructions and the importance of precision.

CHAPTER 9

Using graphics packages

A graphic is how we refer to an image generated by a computer, whether it is a drawing, a diagram, a chart or a photo. Some are created from within programs, such as the graphing function in Excel or the drawing tools in Word. Here we are going to look at programs designed for drawing.

There are lots of graphics packages available with varying degrees of sophistication. 'Granada Colours', for example, is specifically designed for use in schools and includes functions such as 'stamps' or 'symmetry'. Others, such as 'Paintshop Pro' from Jasc or 'Painter' from Corel, were created with graphic designers and other professionals in mind so they therefore have different features including adding effects for lighting or styles such as oil painting or watercolours. However, the basic tools of graphic packages are much the same, any differences being generally in the variations available on those tools.

Using the tools

This is the toolbar from probably the most common graphics program, MS Paint.

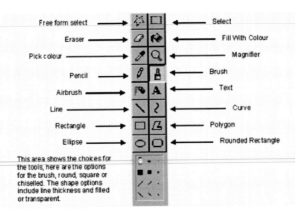

Figure 9.1 *Toolbars in MS Paint*

Most tools are self-explanatory. The **selection** tools are for copying or moving the selected area of the picture to another place. The **magnifier** allows you to work in greater detail, particularly to get rid of the fuzzy edges on drawings. The **colour picker** lets you match a colour on one part of the picture to draw with in another part. The toolbar appears along the side of the screen, the choice of colours at the bottom.

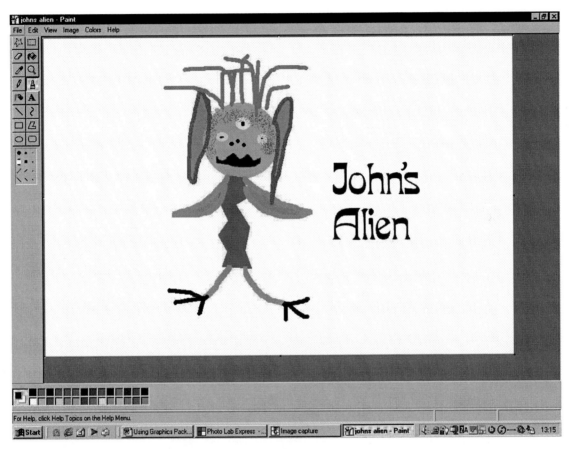

Figure 9.2 *John's alien drawing*

The best way to find out how the tools work is to play with them, swapping tools, options for styles and trying out different aspects of the menus. In MS Paint, the **Image** menu provides a limited number of choices.

Image	Colors	Help
Flip/Rotate...	Ctrl+R
Stretch/Skew...	Ctrl+W
Invert Colors	Ctrl+I
Attributes...	Ctrl+E
Clear Image	Ctrl+Shft+N
✔ Draw Opaque	

Figure 9.3 *The image menu is MS Paint*

An exercise that works well with pupils, which allows them to try out the tools on any graphics package, is to draw an alien. As there is no 'right' answer, they can draw quite freely.

Using drawing programs is a good way to introduce young children to using the mouse, perhaps drawing a wavy line on screen and asking them to trace it with another colour. Here they have to move the mouse with a button held down. If the program has stamps then these can demonstrate how clicking once can cause something to happen. Using the selection tool can help them learn to 'drag and drop'.

Graphics programs are often used with input devices other than the mouse. A 'graphics tablet' is a pad rather like a mouse mat, with a special pen attached. As the user 'draws' on the pad, so the image appears on screen, much more like real drawing than using a mouse.

Many classrooms now have 'touch screens'. These allow you to use your finger instead of the mouse. For young children and those with special educational needs, this immediacy is a good introduction to computer use. Simple exercises, such as writing or tracing their name on screen, can help to develop fine motor control and handwriting skills.

Graphics tools can be used to explore other subjects too. Here the **symmetry** tool in 'Granada Colour' is being used to explore that particular aspect of mathematics by drawing a butterfly.

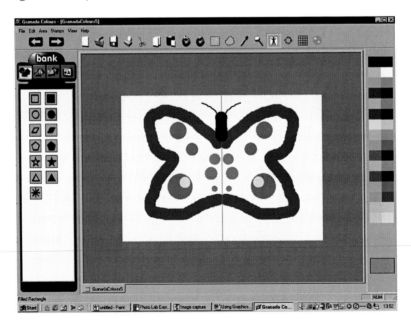

Figure 9.4 *Use of symmetry tool in Granada Colour*

Or the stamps can be used for counting exercises. Here a number of toys have been stamped to make five using the stamps from the library in Granada Colour.

Figure 9.5 *Counting to five*

With older pupils the shape stamps can be used to explore patterns and tessellations.

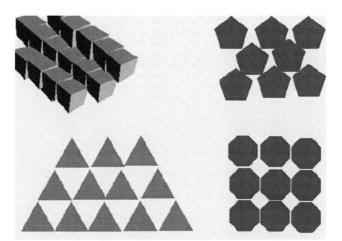

Figure 9.6 *Creating patterns with the stamp tool*

Combining text and graphics

Throughout the ICT curriculum pupils are required to combine text and graphics. In the early stages this could be adding a caption to a drawing, like on 'John's Alien' (Figure 9.2) above. Later on it may be creating a treasure map and pasting it into Word, or creating their own illustrations for a story in PowerPoint.

As with any application, adding a graphic can be done in several ways. If the drawing program is open, it can generally be **copied** from the **Edit** menu then **pasted,** again from the same menu. Or it can be added through the **Insert** menu, following **Insert>Picture>From File** then browsing to find the image.

Using computer graphics can be quite stimulating for pupils as the results can often be more sophisticated than those they can achieve using conventional means such as paper and paint. They also allow them to add colour and explanation to written texts in ways that would be more difficult without the computer.

CHAPTER 10

Using the Internet

The Internet began in the late 1950s as a way for the American military to send messages securely. Any message would be broken into pieces, called 'packets', then sent over a number of routes via a net of communications. If one part of the net was broken the message could travel by other routes, and if any packets were intercepted then the whole message would not be revealed. It still works in much the same way today, bits of information travelling across a network of computers.

The language the Internet uses today, hypertext transfer protocol (the 'http' seen at the beginning of web addresses), was introduced in the early 1990s which is when the Internet began to take off, mainly as a way for academics to share their papers. Nowadays estimates suggest that there are in excess of 3 billion web pages, a lot of which have little educational value (or even non-educational value). There is a lot of very useful information on the Internet and a lot of rubbish. The difficulty can be in sorting one from the other.

Web addresses

There are two ways of finding what you want on the web: typing in an address or doing a search. It is rather like making a phone call – if you know the number you dial it, otherwise you have to look it up or go through directory enquiries.

Web addresses are sometimes referred to as 'URLs' (uniform resource locator) and are typed into the address bar of the 'browser'.

Figure 10.1 *The Internet Explorer browser toolbar*

The address is made up of different segments that each mean something specific, which may let you guess the address of organisations or businesses you are trying to locate. Most, although not all, addresses will begin with 'www' for World Wide Web (you do not need to type in the 'http'). This is followed by the 'domain name', the name the web-site owner has chosen. The last section tells you what type of site it is and what country it originates from, although American addresses do not bother with the country element. These additional elements are known as 'extensions'. Some common extensions are:

- .com – company (.co is the same thing but needs to be followed by a country, such as .uk or .fr)

- .gov – government

- .ac – post-school educational institution, such as a university

- .sch – school

- .org – an organisation, such as a charity

Others include: .biz, .net, .info and .me.
   The country extensions include:

- .uk – United Kingdom

- .nz – New Zealand

- .au – Australia

- .fr – France

- and even .pn for the Pitcairn Islands

The different elements of an address combine to direct users to varying websites. For instance, adding different elements to 'www.canterbury' will take you to a variety of sites. www.canterbury.ac.uk is Christchurch College University of Canterbury but replace the 'uk' with 'nz' (www.canterbury.ac.nz) and you get University of Canterbury in New Zealand. Similarly www.canterbury.gov.uk is Canterbury City Council, but www.canterbury.nsw.gov.au is the local government of Canterbury in NSW, Australia. Other variations include www.canterbury.co.uk (a guide to Canterbury and surrounding areas) and www.canterbury.net.nz/ (web resources to do with Canterbury in New Zealand). As you can see, accuracy is essential when typing in an address.

Another aspect of domain names which it is important to understand is the use of the '~' (the 'tilde'). This is added to addresses to show that they are personal pages hosted by another site, quite often a university. For this reason, any address with a tilde in it should be treated with caution as the views expressed are personal and not necessarily supported by the establishment hosting the pages. By using websites in this way, people with controversial views may be seeking to give an impression of validity. Most such pages are perfectly respectable, but some do need to be treated with caution, such as those used by historians who deny the existence of the Holocaust.

Search engines

If you do not know the address of the site you want, or if you are using the Internet for reference purposes, you will need to use a 'search engine'. This is a website where you type in a 'search term' and get a page, or several pages, of possible results. There are a number of these, such as Yahoo, Altavista and MSN. The most widely used, however, is 'Google', to be found at www.google.co.uk.

Figure 10.2 *Google front page*

As you can see, there are a number of options available when searching. Usually you will type in a word or words then click 'Google Search'. You may want to restrict the search to the UK, or use the 'I'm Feeling Lucky' button which will take you to the most popular page for that search term.

Another useful search tool is the 'Images' tab, which only searches for pictures. To get images for a project on Space, I might type in 'planets' and click 'Google Search'.

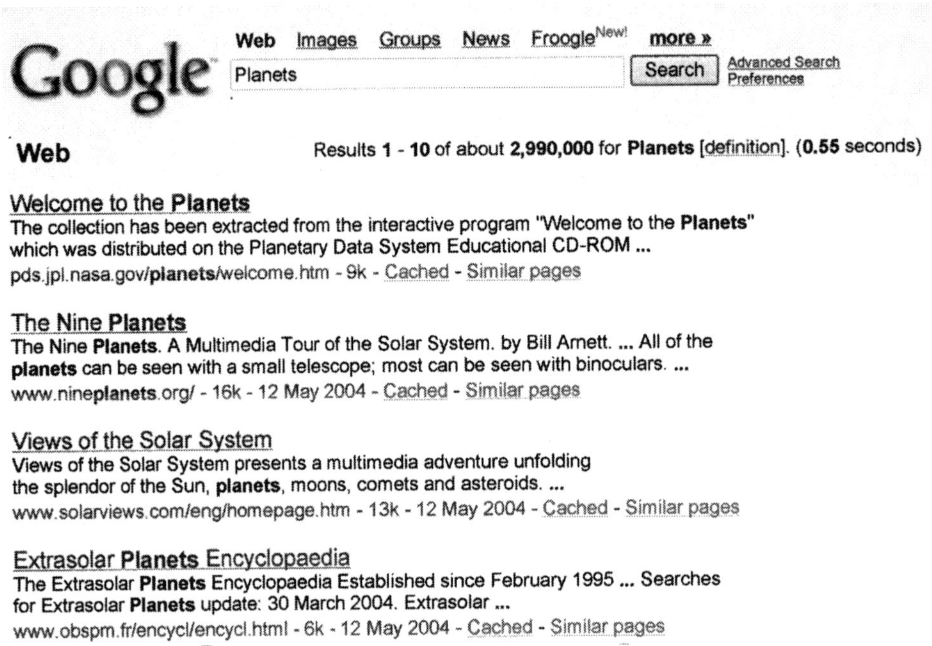

Figure 10.3 *Planets search results*

This gives 'about 66,200' results, or 'hits' (as can be seen in the small print in the middle of this screenshot) each of which is a separate image from a web page. In order to narrow my search down, I need to be more specific, perhaps looking for pictures of a particular planet. However, a search for images of 'Mars' will bring about 990,000 results. Again, being more specific will help.

'Surface of Mars,' brings only just over 2,000, but if I put the phrase in speech marks – 'surface of mars' – I get only 877. This is because Google looks for pages where the search terms occur on the same page, not necessarily all together as a whole phrase. By putting them in speech marks it only gives results where the words appear next to each other. Adding more terms, such as 'NASA', will narrow the results down further – in this case to 217. (The Internet is constantly growing so if you try these searches you will probably get even more results.)

Copyright

When finding images on the Internet it is important to remember that, just like with printed material, they may be copyrighted, so check for copyright information and if you use the image widely, on worksheets for instance, state where it came from. If you publish the image, in a book or on a website, attribute it and get permission to use it from the copyright holder (3-17.2, b).

Figure 10.4 shows the surface of Mars copied from the NASA website where the copyright notice includes, *'Photographs are not protected by copyright unless noted.'*

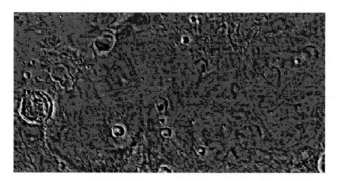

Figure 10.4 *The surface of Mars*

Copying material

To go to a page or image in the results list, simply click on the link to go to it. You will know if a link exists because the cursor changes to a finger, like this, when you move over it.

Figure 10.5 *Browser finger*

Once you have found an image you want to use, the easiest way to copy it is to point at it and **right click,** that is, click with the other mouse button. This brings up a menu of commands. From here simply choose **Copy**, then open or go to the program you are copying into, such as Word or PowerPoint, then **right click** again and choose **Paste.** It is also possible to copy text in a similar way by first of all running the cursor over it to highlight it.

There is a large quantity of material on the Internet, much of it unsuitable for school students. There are a number of ways of restricting access to these pages. In the first instance, school Internet access should be protected either by a 'walled garden' or by 'filtering'. The first of these works by only giving access to websites specified by staff. The problem with this is that the Internet is constantly growing and much valuable material could be missed (3-17.2, c).

You could create a similar system by saving websites into the **Favourites** folder and instructing pupils to only use these sites. To do this, visit the pages you want to include then follow **Favourites>Add to Favourites**, give the page a name or put it in a particular folder, then click **OK.**

Monitoring Internet use

'Filtering' uses a number of ways to check the validity of a web page to determine whether access should be allowed, checking the address and the key words in the text, for instance. For example, pupils could visit the website of 'The Sun' newspaper, but if they tried to view 'Page 3' then a warning would appear saying something like, 'You are trying to access a filtered URL.'

You should also teach children to monitor the Internet themselves and to report any inappropriate pages to an adult. Every school has an 'Internet Acceptable Use' policy which will require staff, pupils and parents to sign a statement about using the web and specifying the sanctions for unacceptable usage. Pupils should also be taught to think about the information they find and its validity, the skills of questioning and discrimination.

Other ways to protect pupils when using the Internet can found at http://safety.ngfl.gov.uk (3-17.2,b). These include:

- monitoring the use of email, particularly web-based mail such as hotmail, perhaps restricting pupils to using class-based addresses;

- restricting the use of chat rooms to educational sites;

- ensuring computer rooms are supervised when pupils are using them;

- because of the risk of viruses, not allowing pupils to download files from the Internet without staff permission.

The Internet can be compared to a library in many respects. Just as a library has rules and expectations of behaviour, so we should set up similar systems for using the web. Pupils should not use it without some sort of supervision, although at secondary age this may be self-monitoring. Do a search yourself before the pupils do so that you can guide them to suitable sites or help them refine their 'search terms'. When they act inappropriately they should be treated accordingly, just as they might be asked to leave a library. The web is a vast resource for education, but one that needs our involvement. We cannot simply leave children to get on with exploring it, just as we would not let them loose in a library without guidance and a clear purpose.

CHAPTER 11

Creating web pages

Creating web pages is easier than it sounds and is increasingly becoming part of the ICT curriculum in schools, as well as being a fun activity for lunchtime or out-of-hours clubs. Web pages are written in a language known as 'HTML' (hypertext mark up language), which is simply a series of commands telling the computer things such as where on the page to place a piece of text, the colours and sizes of fonts, and where to put links to other pages. These commands can be written in any writing program such as MS Word or Notepad. If you want to see what it looks like, open Internet Explorer then, for any web page, follow **View>Source** and the coding will appear in Notepad.

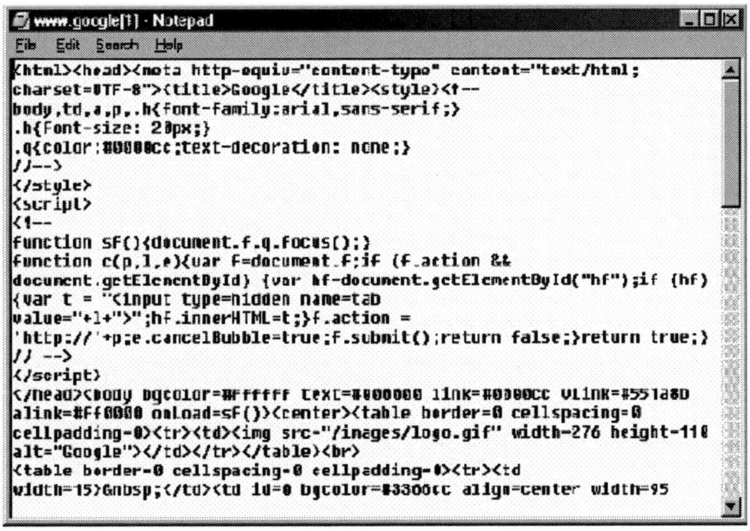

Figure 11.1 *HTML Code for Google home page*

Fortunately you do not have to know any of this to create your own pages. While there are specialist pieces of software such as 'Dreamweaver', 'Front Page' and

'Hotdog Junior', most MS Office programs will also save documents ready to publish straight to the web.

In MS Word, for instance, you simply change the **Save as type:** box to 'HTML Document'. In Ms Publisher the **File** menu includes the option to **Create Web Site from Current Publication**. In PowerPoint the same menu contains the option to **Save as Web Page**. Converting PowerPoint presentations has the added advantage of automatically putting in links between pages as well as preserving any hyperlinks that have been created to other pages or to websites and documents.

Using specialist software such as 'Microsoft Front Page' will let you create a more complex site; however, you will need to learn to use the software as it works a little differently from other programs. The principles will be familiar: place text and images on the page then link them to other pages and other sites.

It can be a bit fiddly remembering to keep saving pages, to give each one a title and to keep checking that your links work as you go. This is because web pages create themselves afresh every time they are opened pulling the various elements together from where they are saved. For this reason all the images you place on a page need to be kept in one folder so that the computer can find them. Secondly each page needs to have its own title and to be similarly kept together in a folder.

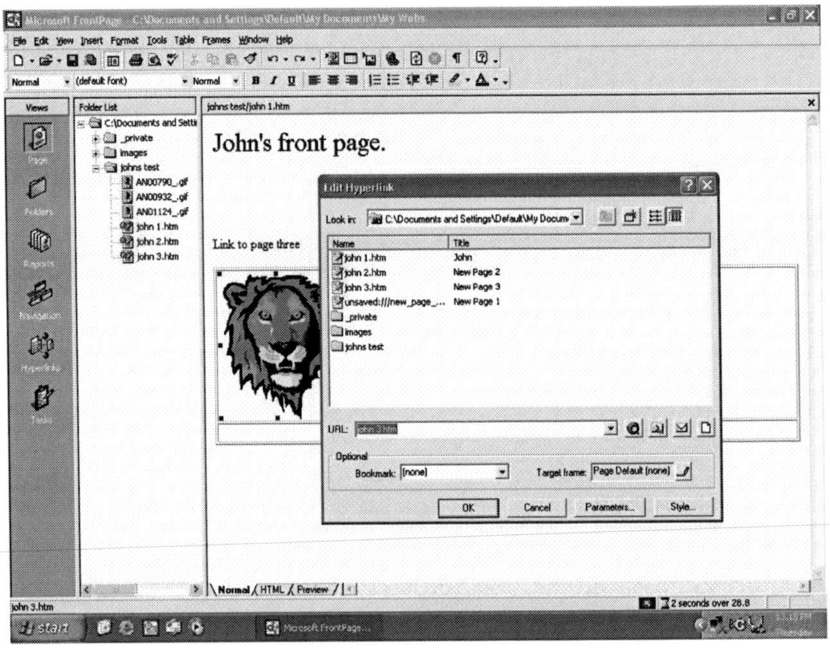

Figure 11.2 *Front page elements*

As you can see from this screenshot, the pages are shown in the left-hand screen (like slides in PowerPoint) and the images are also stored there. The page has a title and a name, and the hyperlinks can be to another page or to a website. At the bottom of the screen are three views: Normal for editing, HTML to see the coding and Preview to try it out. However, you should always open your completed site in a browser such as Internet Explorer to make sure that it works before it is posted on the Internet.

Planning

When creating a web site, whether for your own use or with pupils, it is best to plan in advance what each page will look like, sketching them out and drafting the text, and how they will link together. The pupils can help in this process. Remember, though, that individual users will be able to set their browsers to use different attributes to those you set – font styles and sizes can be changed, for instance – so how you set the page up is not necessarily how users will see it. For this reason it is generally best to keep things simple, using a minimum of font styles and colours. Less complicated pages also load quicker on the Internet.

In designing your web pages, you will also want to consider the balance between text and images. As a very general guide, a web page will comfortably show about 200 words of text without the user having to use the scroll bar to read it.

Using tables is a useful way to organise the content of web pages. You will also come across tools such as 'frames'. This is where the page is broken up into different areas that can be thought of as individual pages. So one area may change independently of another.

Uploading your website

Perhaps the most technical aspect of creating websites is uploading them to the Internet, a process known as FTP (File Transfer Protocol). While this is no different from moving files around on your own hard drive, it is best to get whoever manages the website to do it, as I always do.

CHAPTER 12

Using digital cameras

These very useful devices are becoming increasingly common in classrooms across the country and are being used in a variety of ways. Staff are finding them useful not just for creating records of trips but also to record pupils' achievements and to include in their work. They are particularly useful for small steps in achievement which can be difficult to describe.

They can also be used in lessons for activities such as sequencing. Either the teacher or the teaching assistant can take a series of photos and ask children to put them in order or the pupils can do it for themselves. Even long-term projects such as growing beans or watching tadpoles become frogs can be recorded step by step.

There is a very wide range of cameras on the market, ranging in price from little more than dinner for two to the cost of a new car. In classrooms the quality of the image may matter less than how easy it is to use.

For pupil use, getting the photos off the camera needs to be straightforward. Some cameras come with smart card readers, others connect directly via a special lead. Some use floppy disks or CDs that slip into the appropriate drive. You may also have specific software to move the images between the camera and the computer.

There are a number of things the pupils can do with their photos. One is to edit and enhance them. For this specialist software such as 'Adobe Photoshop' is useful, although most painting programs will open these images so even 'Colour Magic' will let them change the look of it.

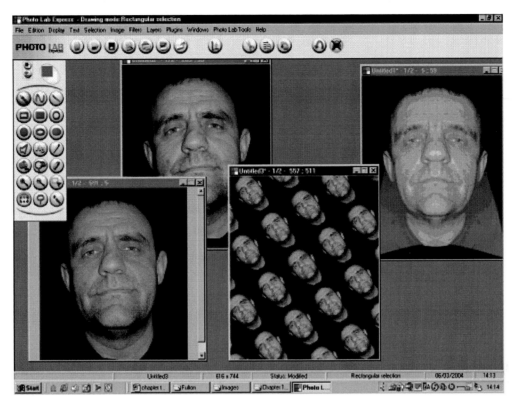

Figure 12.1 *Effects applied to an image*

Another use is as a record of an event or to create a book. Some software that comes with cameras will let you make slide shows very easily, and the latest version of PowerPoint will also do this. Using PowerPoint you can add captions, speech bubbles and backgrounds, and with the printing options available this can be a simple way to create books. Although the options are more restricted than in MS Publisher, it is very straightforward to add an image in PowerPoint. (See Chapter 7 for how to do this.)

If you do not have access to a digital camera, it is still possible to use digital images in the classroom as all ordinary film can be formatted in this way when processed. Simply ask the shop where you get the film developed to create a CD of the images for you for a small extra charge. This way even disposable cameras can become digital ones.

CHAPTER 13

Using a digital video camera

While video cameras have been around for years, it is only recently that we have been able to harness the power of the computer in the classroom to turn that footage into professional-looking films, with fades, credits, soundtracks and effects.

Making movies

Making movies can be great fun and involve a lot of different learning opportunities. There are the obvious ones such as writing a script, as well as the less obvious ones such as working out timings or framing the images. It can also be great for working with groups as pupils can be allocated different roles and responsibilities and they are collectively responsible for the outcome.

The possibilities for films are endless: a video prospectus for the school perhaps, or a record of a school trip. However, you could also use it for pupils to record what they are learning. For instance, a class created a short video in science about 'pneumatics' both to reinforce their learning and to show their parents what they were doing in school. They had to fully understand the subject in order to explain it, which would then be reinforced at home when they talked about it with their families. When making a film, it is often a good idea to start by watching television. Clips from the news make good source material as they convey information in quite a short time. Talk about the different camera angles, the use of close-ups, how long each clip lasts, voice-overs, how the different reporters look at the camera or position themselves when interviewing people.

You will probably want to start quite small as even a five-minute video could take more than an hour of filming to create. Storyboards are very helpful, literally drawing the story like a comic strip to sequence the film and plan the shots. It may be difficult to keep the pupils focused on this – they will understandably just want to get on with it.

Equipment

As well as a digital video camera, it is very useful to also have a tripod, an external microphone and a set of earphones. This is because while it is very tempting to keep the camera moving and to constantly zoom in and out, it is better to keep the camera still (hence the tripod) and to make any changes in focus quite restrained. The external microphone will improve the sound quality and is a useful prop for interviews. The headphones will tell the sound or camera crew whether the reporters or cast can be heard.

Having shot the film, it should be a straightforward procedure to connect the camera to the computer with a 'firewire' lead and let it automatically move the footage across. The film should show up on screen in the segments in which it was shot. When the camera is connected up to the computer, it is possible to record directly onto it.

Editing

Editing software is becoming more common. 'Windows Movie Maker' comes with Windows-based computers (**Start>Programs>Accessories>Windows Movie Maker**) and the highly regarded 'iMovie' comes free with Apple Macintosh computers. Although these latter machines account for only about 10 per cent of computers world-wide, they are the machine of choice throughout the creative industries and it would be worth the school considering buying one. Whichever you use, the computer will need a large memory, as ten minutes of film can take about a gigabyte of space, and you will have both original footage and your edited version stored while working on it.

Apart from the software mentioned, you can also buy specialist titles such as 'Adobe Premiere' or 'Final Cut Pro', which are used by professional film-makers. Whatever you use, they tend to work in similar ways. The screen has three elements: a preview window, another window showing the video clips that have been downloaded from the camera and, at the bottom of the screen, a storyboard showing the clips in order with the effects and transitions showing.

Editing is reasonably straightforward, simply a case of dragging and dropping clips into the timeline. Likewise cutting clips can be done by pulling along the handles at the bottom of the preview window. Effects, such as fading between scenes, are similarly dragged onto the storyboard from a window that replaces the clips one. Credits are added in a similar way.

Viewing your movie

Once you have completed your film, you will need to think about how people will view it. If it is intended to be played on video machines, then you may need to send

Figure 13.1 *The editing screen in Windows Movie Maker*

it back to the camera so that it can be re-recorded on VHS tape on a standard machine. Otherwise you could burn it on a CD or DVD or prepare it to be viewed on the Internet. Some of these require you to save the film in different formats. You can find out about how to do any of these by visiting one of the many websites on this topic. Try the Apple or Microsoft websites – both have tutorials on using their software.

Finally, remember that when creating videos the temptation will be to just get on with it. However, good planning, clarity of purpose, and clear roles and responsibilities all contribute to getting the best results.

PART 3

Background knowledge

CHAPTER 14

Taking control: putting yourself in charge

Always remember who is boss when using technology – even when you are not sure what you are doing, it is still you who has the finger on the 'off' button! There are times when computers do inexplicable things – crashing, freezing, dialling up the Internet, refusing to obey elementary commands, lining up text in the wrong place and refusing to move it. The document you have spent half your life creating (well, a couple of hours anyway) suddenly disappears from the screen. Some of this is beyond our control and we just have to accept that these things happen, but a lot of the time we have more power than we think.

There are two things you need to know: who to ask for help and a bit of basic IT first aid. At school the first of these may be a technician, ICT co-ordinator, class teacher, fellow teaching assistant or even a knowledgeable pupil, depending on what you want to know and how big the problem is. Knowing who to report problems to is required for the knowledge section of the NVQ for Teaching Assistants, unit 3-17. (Criteria 3-17.1,d and 3-17.2,k both refer to this.) A useful way of demonstrating it is to create a flow chart and have the responsible member of staff sign to say that this is correct.

You may also need to make the computer, or other equipment, safe, either by marking it so people know not to use it, or by turning it off. (Again, sections 3-17.1, 6, and 7 require you to show that you do this.)

What you can do about mistakes

Like learning to drive a car, the first thing to do on a computer is to learn how to stop when things start to go in the wrong direction. If you have made a mistake while using a piece of software, you can usually put things right with the **Undo** button. You can also undo by following **Edit>Undo** or simply holding down the **Ctrl** key and pressing **Z**. The drop down arrow beside the button allows you to go

Figure 14.1 *Undo button*

back several steps, often up to 50 should you need to. However, if you go back too far you will probably get very confused about what you have done and just have to start again anyway.

There are also times when software starts to do something that you do not want it to. On a web page you can simply click the **Stop** button. Other times you either have to let it load then close it or go back, or you can try pressing the **Esc** button at the top left of the keyboard. This will sometimes interrupt whatever is happening. However, the main tool in regaining control of your machine once it begins to get out of hand is to hold down the **Ctrl,Alt** and **Del** keys together. This will show you a list of all the programs running, some of which you will not have known were running, and it will usually show you that one has 'Stopped responding'. Click on this program and then on the **End Task** button to close whatever has stopped. Take it easy when you press **Ctrl,Alt** and **Del,** though, as doing it twice may restart, or reboot, your computer.

Having said that though, most problems will be resolved by rebooting the machine. If you have to resort to this, you may lose some work, although it is likely that the program will have an auto recovery function that will automatically show you the document you were working on when it crashed once you get going again. You can then open it and carry on. Something might have gone, but only the last five minutes' worth, not the last five hours'.

Backing up files

The other thing you should do is to save regularly and to back up files, and encourage the pupils to do likewise. Usually in the options for the program, found in **Tool>Options,** there will be an option for automatically saving regularly, so make sure this is set for every five minutes or so. Some programs, MS Publisher for instance, prompt you to save as you go. You can also develop good habits, such as clicking on the **Save** button every so often, or pressing **Ctrl S** (the keyboard shortcut for saving).

Backing up is something that few people seem to do very often, the exception being ICT technicians who will usually back up all the files on the network at least once a week. You should find out what the system is so that you can retrieve old files for pupils or yourself if necessary (one of the 'routines' mentioned in 3-17.2,a). Generally people do not seem to be too bothered about backing up, no matter what our experiences have been of vital documents disappearing into the depths of the machine never to be seen again. However, keeping files in two places is a good thing to do. This can be simply by copying onto CD or floppy disk, or saving copies into web space we may have which we can access from anywhere. Computers can be petulant and it is often when we are working on our most important files that they decide they are not going to co-operate. If you have something backed up, you are no longer beholden to one particular machine and its fickle moods. Strangely it often seems that once you have back-ups organised, you never have to use them.

Checking the power

If a piece of ICT equipment, whether a computer, a printer, a mouse or a video player, refuses to work, the first thing to do is to check that all the leads are pushed in firmly and that the electric socket is turned on. For instance, when the printer will not print, check it has power and that both ends of the printer lead are correctly in place. If you are happy that this is the case and it still will not work, isolate it (pull the plug out) and call the technician (3-17.1, 6, 7 and 3-17.2, 6).

Setting up and installing

There may be occasions when you are responsible for setting up and operating equipment (3-17.1, 2 and 3-17.2, 1), such as the TV and VCR or a laptop and printer for a pupil with SEN such as a visual or physical impairment. Usually this is not a complicated thing to do and you should refer to any instructions provided while doing so (3-17.1, 3). With one or two exceptions, leads are designed to go into only one place (often referred to as a 'port') and they should go in easily. If you have to force them in, then it is probably not the correct port. The ones that may cause confusion because they look the same are the mouse and keyboard, and the speakers and microphone. For this reason these are usually marked with icons or are colour-coded. After setting up equipment you should switch it on and make sure it is set up correctly and working properly (3-17.1, 5 and 3-17.2, j).

Likewise there may be rare occasions when you need to install or re-install software. Again always check with your technical support first as getting it wrong can have big knock-on effects, particularly on networks. However, you may need to run a particular CD-ROM that wants to put files on the computer to make it work properly. In this instance, the 'Installation Wizard' pops up to walk you through the process and it becomes a case of simply clicking **Next** or **I Agree** to the licensing conditions.

If an already installed program stops working, you may want to re-install it. Again this can usually be done simply by inserting the CD and the existing files will be overwritten by the original ones. However, sometimes this gets messy and you may want to uninstall the software to start afresh. Often you will find an

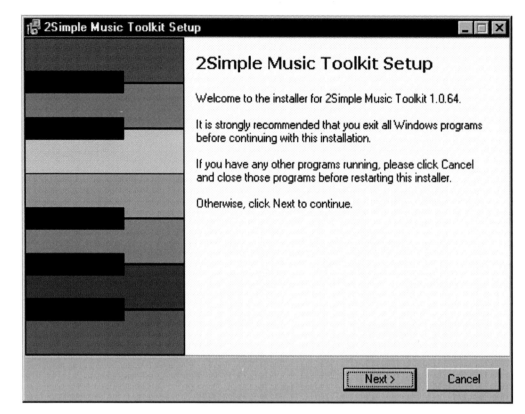

Figure 14.2 *Installation wizard*

option to do this when you open programs from the **Start** menu on the main desktop. However, if there is none, you can uninstall from the control panels. Follow **Start>Settings>Control Panel>Add/Remove Programs.** This will bring up a list of installed software and by clicking on one you will have the option to remove it.

Generally as computer installations in schools become more complex it is best to leave it to those whose job it is to do these things. However, there are some jobs that might fall to anyone, such as replacing the ink and topping up the paper on the printer, and getting out floppy disks and CDs to record work. These are reasonably straightforward and mainly common sense – you may want to be shown the first time but after that it is the kind of thing teaching assistants frequently do in classrooms as recognised by the NVQ (3-17.1,4,c and 3-17.2,7,l). It is even the kind of thing that some of the pupils can do.

What to do if you think a machine might have a virus

All school systems should be protected by virus checkers. They usually run constantly in the background, which means that when you start up the computer they run a quick scan, then scan any file you open, whether from the hard drive, a file server, a floppy disk or CD. They also scan web pages when you open them from

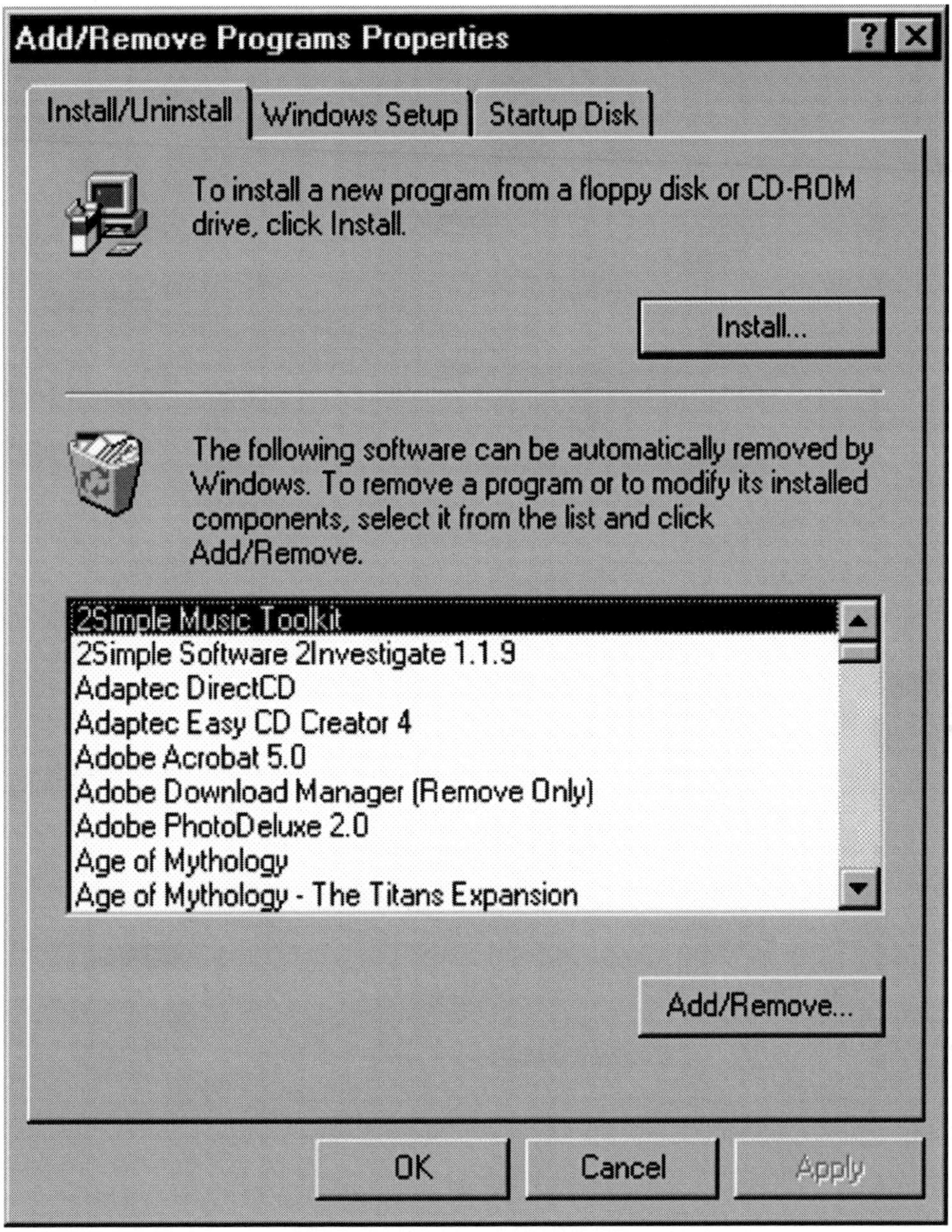

Figure 14.3 *Install/uninstall dialog box*

the Internet, and incoming emails. Even with this level of security you may want to scan individual files or disks separately just to be sure (3-17.2,c).

If you suspect there is a virus on a computer, first of all report it to the ICT co-ordinator or technician. If you have the privileges, run a virus check by double-clicking on the anti-virus software and letting it check the hard drive. The scan should start automatically and, depending on the number of files scanned, quickly report back on how many files have been checked, whether viruses have been found and if it has solved the problem by deleting or quarantining these.

If the problem is with just one file, click once on it to highlight it, open the **File** menu and select the virus check.

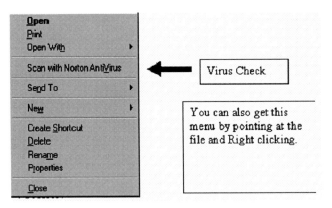

Figure 14.4 *Running a virus check*

Organising files

One thing it is helpful to know is how to organise files on a computer system. The most useful analogy is to think of the computer as an office. The desktop is just that and the filing system is the filing cabinet, its drawers, hanging files and folders. And just like that system it is possible to move things around between them, albeit in an electronic, virtual kind of way.

You may have heard of the hard drive – the permanent memory – in your computer being referred to as the 'C' drive. This is because when computers were first designed they ran off floppy disks, the 'A' drive. When they became more sophisticated and needed two floppy disk drives, 'B' was introduced. When internal disks came about, it was logical that they should be next alphabetically, hence 'C'. As more devices have been added, so the lettering continues. CD and DVD are often, although not always, 'D', 'E' or 'F'. When you get on a network, the different file servers (places to store documents) carry on through the alphabet. Essentially all these different letters represent a place to store files, like the drawers in a filing cabinet. Fortunately the computer will be set up so that there is one common place, like a filing basket, which we will usually use and we do not have to hunt about each time to find the right drive. However, there are times when we might want to save a file elsewhere, on a floppy disk perhaps to take home or to move to a computer that is not on the network.

Ordinarily when you click on **Save As** in the **File** menu, or click the **Save** button on the menu bar, the computer will open a dialog box to put the file in a particular place which can be changed through the 'Save in' box, to a floppy disk perhaps.

The other options when saving are to give the file a name of up to 187 characters (although as a general rule avoid punctuation as this may confuse the machine) and to change the type of file it is, perhaps to an earlier version of the software to use on another machine, or to a different type of document, a web page

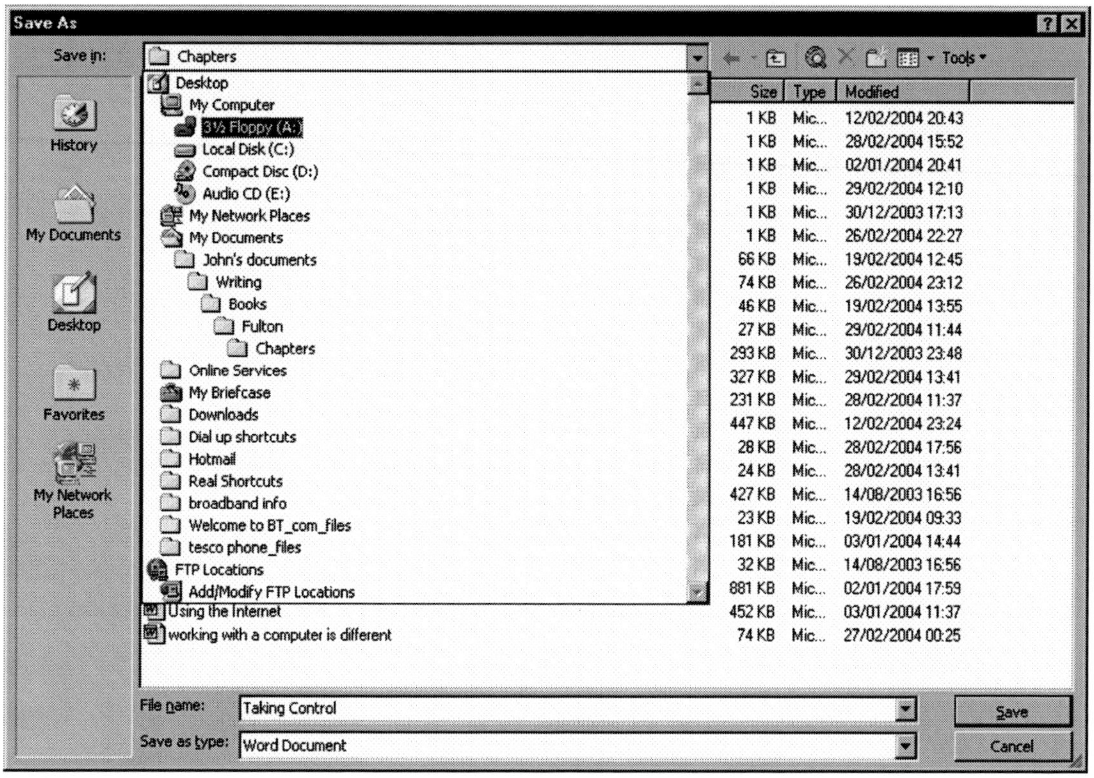

Figure 14.5 *The 'Save As' dialog box*

perhaps. You can also move files around between folders and between drives, both through these dialog boxes and through Windows Explorer. When using Windows Explorer you simply click on a folder to open it and show the folders and files it contains. Again, if it were a filing cabinet you would open the correct drawer, then the folder within it, then the file within that.

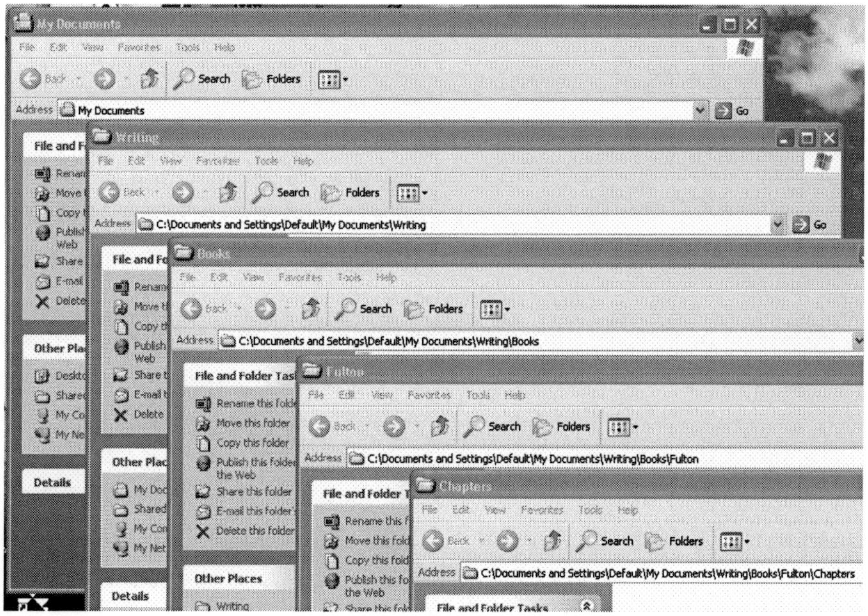

Figure 14.6 *Cascading folders in Windows Explorer*

In this example, you can see this chapter is saved in a folder called 'Chapters' which is itself in one called 'Fulton' which is in one called 'Books,' within 'Writing', in 'John's' contained in 'My Documents'. This sequence is known as the 'file path' and can be seen in the address bar of each folder. The document is located at 'C:\My Documents\John's documents\Writing\Books\Fulton\Chapters'. To move the document to another folder I could either use the 'Edit' menu and **Cut** it and **Paste** it in another folder, or use 'drag and drop' to slide it across the screen. If the new location is on the same drive it will be moved. If it is on another drive, 'A' for instance, it will be copied.

You can use these same techniques for adding files from external devices. Photos from a memory card, for example, can be copied across to your 'My Photos' folder without having to open them in editing software and using 'Save As' to move them.

When working with pupils, you may need to make sure each has their own folder and that their work is saved into it. Primary school networks are often set up with a folder for each class to save work into. At secondary level students are likely to have their own user name and password to log onto the computers, so work is saved automatically into their own space – their network area.

When using networks there are also files that can be shared between users. These may be worksheets to complete or images to use. These areas can also be used for students to save their work for their teachers to mark. (Knowing the details of logging on, what is saved where, and how files can be shared between users are some of the 'operating requirements and routines' you need to know for 3-17.2,a.)

Knowing what to do – becoming intuitive

The difference between computer users who are confident and those who are not is who they blame when things go wrong. The uncertain will assume that it is something they have done – pressed the wrong key, inhaled instead of exhaled, or some genetic disorder that makes them unsuitable to use electrical equipment. The confident user will blame the machine – it is configured wrongly, or built on a Friday afternoon, or not powerful enough to carry out even basic functions. Or they will blame the programmer who designed the software – not intuitive enough, clunky operation, too many clicks, tools are hidden. Sometimes things might go wrong because of something they have done, but they will either see this as a temporary blip until they have learnt how the software works or will simply find a way around the problem.

So the first thing to do to become an intuitive computer user, one who just knows what to do, is to change your attitude. It is not you who is at fault, you can do these things, it is the machine and the way it works that is getting in the way of success.

The second thing is to find what is common between programs. Almost all programs have menu bars, the words that sit at the top of the screen. Quite often the commands within those menus will be the same across all programs. So within the 'File' menu will be the 'Save' command. There will also be a 'Save As' command so you can change the name or type of a file, or keep an earlier version to the one you are working on. The next menu across will almost certainly be the 'Edit' menu where the 'Cut', 'Copy' and 'Paste' commands are located.

The last menu will be the 'Help' menu, which you will quickly learn is usually no help at all, being written in programmer jargon for those who find it difficult to sleep. This means that often you are on your own when learning to use the software because the true title of this menu should be 'Very Little Help'.

This is actually not as bad as it sounds. The way to become an intuitive computer user is simply to play, to explore, to click on each tool and find out what it does and embark on a journey of discovery with each new piece of software you encounter. While this may seem somewhat irresponsible advice, it is this lack of inhibition and inquisitiveness that children bring to computers and that we so often find ourselves jealously admiring. Just remember to keep back-ups and to click **Undo** whenever you get stuck.

The more you use programs, the more you will notice the similarities between them, for example that the 'Active Object' – the one you are working with, whether it is a picture, a chart or a text box – will have black or white dots on the corners and sides, its handles. These can be used to resize it, by holding down the mouse button and dragging. Or it can be moved when the double-headed cross-style cursor appears. You will begin to expect these things and to work with them.

Watch the cursor change to see what sort of action you can take. Is it the browser finger for a link or an arrow to select an object? Take notice of the screen – what is it that changes when you take certain actions? When you get a box pop-up to give you information, read it even when you may not know what it means. It might one day make sense.

Finally, ask how something is done. Confident people see others using programs and they want to know how they did what they just did. Users who are comfortable with computers are not uncomfortable about not knowing. They realise that no individual can know it all, so they exchange tips all the time. Not knowing is not a problem, but not asking is.

Doing it differently

Part of behaving like a confident computer user is doing things a bit differently. We can all point at buttons on the menu bar and click to get a command, but few of us use either keyboard commands or the right mouse click. These are both faster to use than the standard method of pointing and clicking.

There are at least six different ways to cut and paste. Ring the changes to choose one that suits your way of working. For all of them, start by highlighting the text then select from:

1. Open the edit menu and choose **Cut**. Move the cursor, open the edit menu and choose **Paste**.

2. Click on the **Cut** button. Move the cursor and click on the **Paste** button.

3. **Right click**. Choose **Cut**, move the cursor, **right click** and choose **Paste**.

4. Hold down **Shift** and press **Delete**. Move the cursor, hold down **Shift** and press **Insert**.

5. Point at the highlighted section. Hold down the left mouse button. Drag the selection to where you want it.

6. Hold down **Ctrl** and press **X.** Move the cursor, hold down **Ctrl** and press **V.**

7. Any combination of the above.

The last but one of these, using what are known as 'keyboard short cuts', is one of the quickest ways of working as you do not have to move your hand from the keyboard to the mouse. You can even highlight the text with the keyboard just by holding down the **Shift** key then using the navigation arrows at the side of the keyboard to move it across the text.

Keyboard short cuts are very useful for pupils with fine motor difficulties. They can do what they want without having to click accurately, manipulate the mouse pointer into position with a button held down, or click or double click while keeping it quite still.

There are a number of ways of finding these short cuts. One is to hold down the **Ctrl, Shift** and **Alt** keys singly and in combinations and press every other key on the keyboard to see what effect it has. The other is to look in the menus where they are listed beside the commands. You can also find them through the 'Help' files.

Edit	View	Insert	Format
↰	Undo Typing	Ctrl+Z	
↻	Repeat Typing	Ctrl+Y	
✂	Cut	Ctrl+X	
📋	Copy	Ctrl+C	
📋	Office Clipboard...		
📋	Paste	Ctrl+V	
	Paste Special...		
	Paste as Hyperlink		
	Clear	▶	
	Select All	Ctrl+A	
🔍	Find...	Ctrl+F	
	Replace...	Ctrl+H	
	Go To...	Ctrl+G	

Figure 14.7 *Edit menu with short cuts showing*

One very useful one is **Ctrl** and square brackets [or]. When text is highlighted and you use these, the size of all the text changes by one point. So if different sizes have been used, the proportional difference between them all is preserved. Try it. People are always impressed.

To use the **Right Click** commands, simply click once with the right mouse button which will bring up a menu of commands dependent upon which program you are using. This menu, from MS Word, gives standard formatting options along with a list of synonyms for the word that the cursor is in.

Doing things your own particular way on a computer is an indication that you are controlling it rather than it controlling you. The more you learn to do this, the more you will think and feel a confident, skilled, intuitive user.

Figure 14.8 *Right click menu*

Talk the talk

You also need to sound like a skilled user. It is important when working with pupils that, as far as possible, you use the correct language. In part this is so that you and they are clear about the learning that is happening (3-17.2,d), as words provide the framework on which to hang the concepts they have learnt. They allow them to talk about the subject accurately and are a useful tool for assessment. If the language of the subject is used correctly, it is a clear indication that learning has taken place.

When working with pupils, explicitly teach the language of the subject. Every scheme of work should include key vocabulary. When using spreadsheets, this might include, 'cell', 'model', 'formula' and 'reference'. Ask the pupils for definitions then explain the additional meanings. For example, as well as being a place to keep prisoners, a 'cell' is also part of a living organism and more crucially one of the spaces on a spreadsheet. An 'address' is where you live as well as where you will find a particular web page. In this case you could also use the term 'URL' (for 'Uniform Resource Locator') which is a more accurate term that older pupils should understand even if they do not use it often.

If you are not sure what the key vocabulary is, you should ask the class teacher, or you could look it up. Most schools work with schemes of work issued by the QCA. These can be found on the Internet at their website www.qca.org.uk. Even if a school is not using these schemes, they will still give some idea of the language of the topic. These can be put on posters on the wall and given out to learn as spellings for homework. For example, here is some of the vocabulary children might encounter in Year 3:

- database
- field
- record
- file
- sort
- classify
- order
- chart
- simulation

When they get to Year 7 they will also need to know:

- address
- cell reference
- value
- variable

Some computer terms are difficult to define, such as 'value', again from spreadsheet work. If this is the case, look it up. While it might mean how much we will pay for something, it is, according to *Webster's NewWorld Dictionary of Computer Terms*, 'a number entered into a spreadsheet cell'. You can also use the Internet where there are several websites offering this resource. However, ideally the classroom or school library will have a specialist dictionary of computer terms. It is well worth investing in one.

To be a confident and competent computer user, act like one, talk like one and as you get to know them better develop a greater understanding of what they really can do and a healthy scepticism about much of what it is claimed they will do.

CHAPTER 15

What is good ICT teaching?

There are a couple of occasions when your work with pupils might come under scrutiny. One is when Ofsted come visiting. The other is during your assessment for the NVQ.

Like it or not, the judges of what constitutes a good school in this country are Ofsted. What they want to see is both good teaching of ICT and good use of ICT in teaching and learning across the curriculum. So what do they look for?

For a start Ofsted look at the entire educational provision within a school, which includes teaching assistants. While it is unlikely that an inspector would observe you directly and comment on your work, it is possible. However, what they are most interested in is how you work within the classroom, how you work with the class teacher to deliver the curriculum, and how what you do with groups or individuals fits in with the learning intentions of the lesson. This is as true in ICT as in every other subject.

Most of what they will look for is common sense and likely to be how you work anyway. They will want to see that teachers have some idea of what pupils already know; how the lesson they observe fits into the broader scheme of work; that the learning intentions are clear and are known by the pupils; how well they engage with the learning; and that there are opportunities built into the lesson to check that learning is happening.

Planning for inspection

The lesson needs to be well planned, although this does not mean that if a fruitful learning opportunity offers itself this cannot be pursued. Your role should be clear – who you are working with and how. If this is not the case, do clarify it with the class teacher, particularly as it is the sort of thing an inspector might ask about.

It is quite possible that the lesson is based on the scheme of work developed by the QCA, as this provides a good benchmark for the curriculum. If it is not then the school needs to show that the work pupils are doing is just as challenging and rigorous and that the National Curriculum is being sufficiently well covered.

The inspectors will also be looking to see how well the pupils work with the ICT, both in the subject area and in other lessons. Are they confident? Do they have a positive approach? Are their skills appropriate to their age group?

While typing up a smart copy of an essay from their workbooks to the computer can produce a room full of young people quietly tapping away and engaged in the task, it is not necessarily good ICT teaching. If all they are doing is transferring the text from one medium to another and the exercise is merely to provide smart copies to stick on the wall, you have to wonder what is wrong with their hand-writing? If, on the other hand, they are working from notes or a plan, developing their work as they go and using formatting features, such as changing font attributes or adding clip art, then they are harnessing the benefits of using a computer.

If the same result could have been achieved other than with a computer, then think about why the machine is being used. If it is just to show that computers are used in the classroom, then it is better not to demonstrate it that way.

If you do find an inspector in your classroom and that your work is under scrutiny, you may well, like thousands of others, find this stressful. It is an out-of-the-ordinary situation in which you will feel that your actions and your work are being judged. However, if you make sure you know what the aims of the lesson are and what the learning intentions are for any particular pupils with whom you are working, and are comfortable with using the technology and talking to your charges about it, you should come out the other side with a useful experience under your belt (or at least a reason to party come Friday).

NVQ observation

Doing the NVQ could be good preparation for this as it will involve at least one observation. This could cover most of the Performance Indicators for both 3-17.1 and 3-17.2 (as well as a few for other units). Your assessor might specifically look for how you give instructions, guidance and support (3-17.2,d,2,3); that you are comfortable with the software and know what the pupils should be using (3-17.2,e,f); that you know what skills pupils should have at their age and that you help to develop them (3-17.2,g,h,i); and very importantly that you 'provide a level of assistance to enable pupils to experience a sense of achievement, maintain self-confidence and encourage self-help skills in the use of ICT' (3-17.2,4).

You will probably find this stressful too. However, any such observation will be discussed with you in advance; it will be clear what the assessor is looking for and what you will be doing; and the feedback will be based on that. Even if you do not get it quite right, you will probably be given another opportunity.

CHAPTER 16

Health and safety issues

Despite the fact that we come across them everywhere and use them all the time, computers can be bad for your health, although those at risk are mainly people who use them all day every day because they are an integral part of their work. In schools this is not yet the case. Problems identified include physical ones such as repetitive strain injury (RSI) or backache, eye strain and headaches. Much of the risk can be removed or reduced by setting up our working space properly, taking breaks and doing exercises.

Although school staff and pupils may be at less risk than others, adopting some of these practices will make working with a computer easier and reduce any associated discomfort. Computer workstations in schools are generally for multiple users so they will not always suit everybody. However, some generalisations can be made and where possible the set-up should be flexible.

Key points for working at the computer

- The user should be able to sit at the computer with their feet flat on the floor, their knees lower than their buttocks.

- The forearm should be at the same height as the keyboard, so that when typing it is either parallel to the floor or sloping slightly downward.

- Wrists should be held up, and flat or curved slightly downwards. A wrist rest can be used to achieve this. Hands should not bend upwards from the wrist.

- There should be about a hand's width between the keyboard and the edge of the desk.

- The top of the monitor should be level with or slightly below eye level and able to be tilted by the user for comfort. It should be about 45 cm to 50 cm from the user.

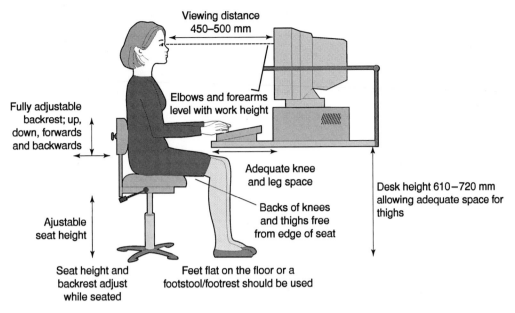

Figure 16.1 *Sitting properly at a workstation*

The computer should be placed in a position where there is no reflection on the screen, although changing the angle of the monitor can solve this. Computer suites, designed for the purpose, are often better set up than classroom computers which are sometimes placed where the trolley fits best, or a socket is available, rather than where the risks of discomfort are minimised.

Children, particularly younger ones, may have to crane their heads back to look up to the screen then down again to pick out the letters on a keyboard. There may be insufficient space to put books or paper down beside the keyboard to work from, and glare from overhead lighting or windows can make the screen difficult to see.

Computers in classrooms can take up a lot of space, and the furniture used, even trolleys designed for the purpose, does not always allow for this. Ideally chairs should be adjustable with no arms and the type of back that supports the lumbar region.

It may be, with some creative thinking, that these situations can be improved. Using higher chairs and providing footrests for small children will lift them up. Often the monitor is placed on top of the hard drive – can this be moved to the side or underneath the table, or even sit on a shelf on the wall? If necessary pull the table out from the wall and let the monitor overhang the back of it (make sure it is safe).

Likewise space can be created by moving the printer to another place and buying a longer printer lead. Glare can be reduced by positioning the computer elsewhere, by lowering a blind or even creating a hood from sugar paper to sit around the top of the screen. A document holder attached to the monitor will not only give pupils somewhere to put work, but also minimise head movements.

Apart from promoting good posture while sitting at the computer, other good practice would include taking regular breaks (five minutes every hour as a general guide) and developing good keyboard skills. Touch typing and using keyboard short cuts can both reduce strain on the limbs. As mentioned previously, keyboard short cuts allow you to use commands through the keys rather than the mouse such as **cut (Ctrl X)**, **copy (Ctrl C)**, **paste (Ctrl V)**, **print (Ctrl P)** or **save (Ctrl S)**.

Health and safety rules

Should anything break down or become damaged, you need to know what to do about it. Your priority must be the safety of the children and your colleagues. Your school will have health and safety procedures for you to follow. These will include common sense instructions such as to turn equipment off and disconnect it from the mains. You may want to warn other users by labelling faulty equipment, or even prevent them from using it by removing the mains lead (3-17.1,6,7, 3-17.2,8).

When you are sure the equipment can be safely left, you will need to report the fault. Most schools will have a system of reporting things in writing, although this can sometimes just be a word with the responsible person during break. However, try to keep a written record as this allows you to keep track of what has happened and what has been done about it (3-17.1,d, 3-17.2,6,k).

There are some tasks, such as changing the bulb in the overhead projector or changing the printer cartridge, that you might want to do yourself (3-17.1,4,c, 3-17.2,7,l). However, for more complex problems it is generally best to leave things to those whose job this is.

Internet safety and child protection

It is not only how computers are set up that has safety implications, but also how they are used. The Internet can be a great tool for learning and a useful addition to the teaching toolbox. However, it is largely unregulated, meaning that almost anyone can communicate through it, both directly through chat and email, and indirectly by publishing web pages.

As responsible adults, those of us working in classrooms need to be aware of the problems inherent in such an open medium and what we can do to look after children. Some of the concerns about Internet use raise issues of child protection (3-17.2,b).

There are four areas of Internet use that we need to consider:

- the nature of the information that pupils may encounter
- posting information on school websites

- the use of email by pupils

- chat rooms

When we connect to the Internet we do so through an Internet Service Provider (ISP). Often schools will use one dedicated to education who will provide a filtering service for web content. This means that any web page a pupil opens will have been screened to ensure that its content is appropriate. These tend to work by stopping information from particular addresses, looking for key words on web pages or in addresses, and by checking pages against a data base of proscribed sites (see Chapter 10).

Another approach used by schools is known as the 'walled garden'. Here pupils are only allowed access to a specified list of sites. These approaches are only partial solutions. The restricted access of a walled garden may mean that some useful sites are not included. As the Internet is growing all the time, it will be necessary to continually review the content to make sure up-to-date pages are included.

A filtering approach may still allow pupils access to sites with dubious content. For example, a search on 'multi-ethnic education' may give access to racist, white supremacist sites that are opposed to the concept. Filtering also offers a challenge to some pupils to find ways around it.

Generally if pupils are doing research on the Internet you will want to provide some guidance. Depending on the age of the pupils, this may range from directing them to particular pages to discussing the information found and how we can determine what is valid.

Your school should have an Acceptable Use Policy for the Internet which will outline what is acceptable behaviour and state what to do if inappropriate sites are accessed (3-17.2,c).

If your school has a website, it will also have a policy on what can be published, or posted, on the site. One major concern will be to prevent the identification of children. If photos are used careful thought needs to be given to the appropriateness of the content. Parental permission should also be gained before posting. This could be done as part of the arrangements at the beginning of the year when home/school agreements and similar commitments are being made. As a general rule pupils under 16 should not be readily identifiable. If a pupil is in a photo, do not put their name in the caption. Likewise, do not give forename, surname or class as these can be used to single out a specific child.

One reason for such precautions is that identification may allow a child to be contacted through email. Again your school needs a clear policy on what addresses are used, what level of access to email pupils have and when it can be used. Some schools may provide all pupils with email addresses, while others might only provide one address for a class to use collectively. Guidance for email use might include:

- All pupil email in school is public, that is, open for anyone to read.

- Only email accounts provided by the school should be accessed.

- No access should be given to web-based mail such as that provided by Hotmail or Yahoo.

- No personal details should be included in messages.

Depending on the age and maturity of the pupils, the school may also want to limit email use to a closed system, that is one that is only accessible to users from the same school or educational community, such as that being provided on large education networks like the London Grid for Learning.

Similar concerns are also raised by pupil use of chat rooms. There are a number of chat rooms that are educationally focused. Good ones will be moderated, that is they will have someone monitoring the conversation to make sure that nothing untoward is said or that personal details are not exchanged. When using a chat room pupils need to be clear what the educational purpose is. What is it that they are trying to find out or discuss? Just as pupils would not be allowed time for general conversation during lessons, so their use of chat rooms on the Internet should also be restricted to learning-based activities.

CHAPTER 17

Legal knowledge

There is not a great deal about ICT and the law that you need to know in your role as a TA working in classrooms. However, you need some understanding of a few key areas: data protection, copyright and licensing (3-17.2,b).

Data Protection Act

You will need to bear this Act in mind in the course of your work, although it is unlikely you will need to refer to it specifically. Just be aware of the basic provisions.

The Data Protection Act covers all instances when data is collected. It has eight principles which say that data must be:

- fairly and lawfully processed;
- processed for limited purposes;
- adequate, relevant and not excessive;
- accurate;
- not kept longer than necessary;
- processed in accordance with the data subject's rights;
- secure;
- not transferred to countries without adequate protection.

In the classroom you will probably be handling data for two purposes:

- maintaining pupil records
- curriculum work

In the first of these tasks, you might be contributing to the record of pupils' achievements in school. This could be through discussion with class teachers; through keeping records of groups you are responsible for; and through contributions, in writing or at meetings, on pupil progress. This latter might include annual reports or reviews for pupils with special educational needs.

In curriculum work, you may be collecting information for data handling. This could take many forms, but might include personal pupil information from such things as shoe size to number of people in the family or distance they live from school.

The application of the principles is largely common sense and will contribute to good practice in schools. When thinking about pupil records, it means that comments or notes you make should be fair, based on fact and kept for a reason. They should be dated and attributed, that is, it should be clear who has made the record and when.

Obviously there are times when you will be asked for an opinion – how a child is getting on with classmates, for instance – but you will base your reply on clear evidence, what you have seen happening in the playground perhaps. Any written notes you make should have your name and date on them. Bear in mind that not only can parents request to see educational records, but so can pupils. So make sure that they are fair and clear.

When working on classroom tasks with pupils, consider what information can be shared. Pupils may be sensitive about certain information but this is more about good practice than data protection. It is unlikely, for instance, that you would collect data on household income, unless for a specific project, in geography perhaps, and then it could be done in such a way that individuals' rights to privacy were protected. Likewise if you were looking at how pupils got to school you would use home addresses as part of the work, although you would not give them out to pupils to use for homework.

Overall data protection is about common sense and individual rights to privacy and fairness. Your school should have a member of staff designated to deal with data protection issues, usually a member of the Senior Management Team, so anything you are not sure of can be dealt with by them.

Copyright

Copyright is intended to make sure that an individual's efforts are not exploited by others through unauthorised use. It broadly covers anything that is created and published, whether it is a book, a song, an image, a computer program or a website, and is meant to ensure that any earnings go to the creator along with the due acknowledgement of their work and ideas.

This does not mean that every time you use someone else's work you have to ask their permission. Generally schools are covered by the Copyright Licence Agreement (CLA) which allows for limited copying for specific purposes.

However, the CLA does not cover electronic materials presented on CD-ROM, floppy disk or websites. The tools computers provide can make the unauthorised use of material published in this way much easier.

Some files, such as clip art, are authorised to be used by others, although the copyright will remain with the creator. This means that you can use the images, for making a worksheet or poster perhaps, but should acknowledge the source if you distribute them more widely, outside the school for instance, and should not pass them off as your own.

Other resources, such as CD-ROMs and websites, are also covered by copyright and there is usually a statement making clear whose intellectual property they are. Again this may include a statement about what can be used, by whom and for what purposes. The Encarta website has many articles that can be used for individual study which include the following information:

How to cite this article:
Microsoft® Encarta® Online Encyclopedia 2004

The Plain English Campaign provides downloadable guides on using plain English on its website. It makes clear, however, that:

Plain English Campaign owns the copyright on all of these guides. You are welcome to print out any of the guides or save them to disk for your own use. You may not photocopy any guide or pass on electronic copies without permission.

(http://www.plainenglish.co.uk/guides.html)

Just as with printed texts, there are guidelines as to what can be copied from the Internet. Generally you can, for instance:

- Print out a web page for study or research, although no more than 1 per cent of a site can be reproduced.

- Make a single copy of a web page, although not the whole site, to a hard drive or disk, as long as it is not used for making multiple copies.

- Quote from a web page as long as the source is acknowledged.

- Make a temporary copy of a file or web page for the purposes of electronic transmission, for email, for instance.

You should not, however, reproduce information from one web page on your own pages without the permission of the copyright holder, although you could provide a link.

There is also, of course, the problem of plagiarism – students copying material from the Internet and passing it off as their own. This is difficult to detect unless the work is significantly different from usual. Signs might include the use of

American spellings or unusual phrasing, especially if they have lifted it straight out of an online encyclopaedia. It is always good practice to talk to children about their work as one way of checking whether they have learnt the topic or just copied it. Another possibility is to do a web search on a key phrase from the essay to see what comes up.

Licensing

We often talk about licences for computer software. Whether it is installed on the hard drive, run from a CD or floppy disk, or downloaded from the Internet, most of what we use will have conditions attached to its use. The licence specifies what those conditions are.

This is because when you use software, ownership of the program remains with the copyright holder. You have the right to use it in particular ways laid down by the owner. Typically a licence will specify how many users or computers the software can be run on. It is permissible for users to make one copy of a program for back-up purposes. However, this copy should not then be run on unlicensed machines.

- A 'single user licence' means the program can be installed and run on only one machine.

- A 'site licence' allows it to be used on any machine on a given site, so a split site school would probably need two site licences.

- A 'network licence' allows for the use of the program across a network of connected computers, although it may specify the maximum number of computers it can be run on.

- A 'concurrent licence' lets the software be installed on any number of machines, although only a given number of users can run it at any one time.

In practice the programs you use in the classroom will be licensed when they are purchased and either the ICT co-ordinator or a member of the Senior Management Team will ensure that the terms of any agreements are adhered to.

Licensing agreements are important to protect the rights of the copyright owner to their intellectual property and to any income derived from it. It is also important for schools because institutions that are in breach of licensing agreements can be heavily fined, and individuals found to be illegally copying or using software can be disciplined and even dismissed.

It is unlikely that you will ever have legal difficulties when using ICT in school. Your common sense will aid you to a large degree. However, if you are not sure, check with someone who should know. When in doubt, do not do it.

CHAPTER 18

Getting qualified

The roles of the various adults in classrooms are changing with the moves to remodel the education workforce. As part of this initiative, there is an increased emphasis on having not just qualified teachers but also qualified teaching assistants.

While the current changes will see support staff undertake traditional teacher tasks, the reforms are about more than delegating jobs and are intended to reframe their role, including developing the post of Higher Level Teaching Assistant. Working under the direction of the classroom teacher, this new post will increase teaching assistant involvement in planning, delivery and assessment of learning.

The current LGNTO standards are based on good practice, drawn up through broad consultation, and cover a range of jobs in all types of school, whether staff are working with specific children, offering general classroom support, or even if they have particular subject or age group responsibilities. While one constant is that all school staff work with pupils with SEN at some time, the diverse range of roles teaching assistants fulfil is difficult to compare, hence the 28 sections of the guidance.

The NVQ for teaching assistants

The National Vocational Qualification (NVQ) or Scottish Vocational Qualification (SVQ) comes directly from the National Standards. These offer teaching assistants the opportunity to have their skills recognised with an accredited qualification regardless of the job they do. Level 2 has four mandatory units and three optional ones, while Level 3 has four mandatory units and six optional. The units are built around different aspects of the work, including using ICT, managing behaviour and preparing the learning environment. The expectations vary between the two levels, so the difference is more than just the amount of units covered.

The advantage of the S/NVQ is that it is based on a range of evidence, dependent on an individual's position. Unlike more traditional qualifications, there is no course as such, nor specified examinations or coursework. The teaching assistant takes the main responsibility for moving the qualification on through the portfolio they compile, supported by their assessor and their school mentor. The involvement of the school in evaluation means their achievement is fully understood at work.

To complete an NVQ you would need to gather together a portfolio of evidence to demonstrate certain things. As mentioned in the introduction, the ICT unit has two elements:

3-17.1 Prepare ICT equipment for use in the classroom

3-17.2 Support classroom use of ICT equipment

which have been referenced where relevant throughout this book. Each element has criteria (broken down into what you need to show and what you need to know), as well as a scope of equipment and skills that each applies to.

Each candidate has an assessor who will help to plan how they will be assessed and what evidence to gather for the portfolio. This might include attending courses, answering verbal or written questions and keeping a record of work with pupils. The assessor will also want to observe you. Generally the performance indicators headed 'You must show' will need to be observed. However, this can be through role play and simulation. Examples of evidence you will use are:

- witness statement from the teacher/SENCO

- records of observation by assessor

- written questioning/project work

- records of professional discussion

- health and safety records

- differentiated instruction manuals produced by candidate

- example of learner's work with annotated commentary

Within the unit, one piece of evidence can cover a number of criteria and any piece of evidence can be used for more than one unit. While the necessary cross-referencing is a time-consuming task, it will speed up gaining the qualification in the end.

Pre-S/NVQ

Teaching assistant professional development now begins with a DfES-prescribed induction course which has eight half-day modules that look at: role and context; behaviour management; supporting literacy and numeracy; and special needs and inclusion. During the course students compile a portfolio. This portfolio can then provide evidence for accredited courses, either the Level 2 S/NVQ or a similar course at the same level such as 'Supporting Teaching and Learning' from OCR. This is a useful introduction to these assessment methods. Evidence is compiled around four units of work and assessed in conjunction with the school.

Post-NVQ

For most teaching assistants, achieving the S/NVQ will be sufficient recognition of their professional capabilities. Others may wish to proceed further, perhaps to Qualified Teacher Status. This will only be a few, as most do not want to be running the classroom and are happy in a supporting role. Foundation degrees are available for those who want to go further as is the Higher Level Teaching Assistant qualification.

A foundation degree is a vocationally based qualification equivalent to the first two years of a bachelor's degree. It requires a greater level of reflection and a deeper understanding than the S/NVQ. There is a website dedicated to foundation degrees at http://www.foundationdegree.org.uk.

These qualifications do not have standard descriptions so it is necessary to have a good look for all the relevant ones. They can be searched by region and with over 100 available for teaching assistants there is likely to be something local.

What else is there?

There is sufficient flexibility in the qualifications system to acknowledge specific expertise or interests, such as the use of ICT. For example, London Metropolitan University currently offers 'Making use of ICT: Primary Classroom and Early Years Support Staff', which gives 15 CATS (Credit Accumulation and Transfer Scheme) credits that can be put towards a final qualification. Pearson Publishing are offering 'Using ICT to Support Learning' with a new version specifically for SEN pupils. OCR have recently developed the Certificate in Information and Communications Technology for Teachers and Trainers. Whenever embarking on a course, it is always worth trying to find something of genuine interest to keep you motivated when the going gets difficult.

Further information

There is a wealth of information available on the Internet on all aspects of this book. Below are some of the key sites.

Teaching and learning

www.dfes.gov.uk The website for the Department of Education and Science.

www.becta.org.uk This is the lead agency for ICT and education in England. Loads of useful advice and information, including online interest groups, advice sheets and the Communication Aids Project (CAP) area for ICT and SEN.

www.nc.uk.net National Curriculum website where you can find useful links, resources and schemes of work.

www.qca.org.uk The body responsible for the curriculum and assessment.

www.safety.ngfl.gov.uk A DfES site that provides guidance on safe Internet use.

www.tes.co.uk The Times Educational Supplement hosts a forum for teaching assistants in its 'Staffroom' area.

ICT and SEN

The Inclusion website provides information on resources and advice for practitioners at http://inclusion.ngfl.gov.uk. Information about many aspects of ICT and SEN including adapting ICT resources can be found at the ACE Centre site http://www.ace-centre.org.uk/html/resources/resource.html. There is useful information about SEN ICT resources at the website of Inclusive Technology, part of Granada Learning at www.inclusive.co.uk.

Some organisations have sites about specific aspects of SEN:

www.bda-dyslexia.org.uk The British Dyslexia Association.

www.nas.org.uk The National Autistic Society.

www.rnib.org.uk The RNIB.

www.rnid.org.uk The RNID.

www.drc-gb.org The Disability Rights Commission have lots of information.

Getting qualified

The LGNTO standards can be found at http://www.lg-employers.gov.uk. Further information about S/NVQ courses, including syllabuses, can be found from the websites of the awarding bodies. They are:

The Council for Awards in Children's Care and Education (CACHE)

www.cache.org.uk or phone 01727 847636.

City and Guilds

www.city-and-guilds.co.uk or phone 020 7294 2800.

Oxford, Cambridge and RSA Examinations

www.ocr.org.uk or phone 024 7647 0033.

The Scottish Qualifications Authority

www.sqa.org.uk or phone 0141 242 2214

Evidence for the NVQ

Listed below are the competences for 'Support the Use of ICT in the Classroom' with page references for where information about each one appears in this book. (There are couple of omissions left blank because these will be particular to your situation and are therefore difficult to generalise about.)

For 3-17.1, a,b and 3-17.2 9,m you need to know what sorts of ICT equipment your school has, how they are booked out and how they are kept safe. This can be a straightforward written report, or even covered through answering questions.

The other criterion 3-17.2,4 is central to your work. It is about pupils' personal learning experiences and will need to be observed by your assessor. While this book may have shown you how you can use ICT effectively in your work, this one is about your working relationships with your pupils. No matter how good you are with the ICT, unless you have these skills for working with young people you will not be effective in your role.

At the end of each section is the 'Scope'. This shows the breadth of activities and knowledge you need to have evidence for. You do not need to cover all the scope for each criterion, but you need to satisfy the assessor that they are covered across the unit as a whole.

Standard 3-17.1: Prepare ICT equipment for use in the classroom

Performance indicators	
You must show that you:	**Page no.**
1. Confirm the requirements for ICT equipment with the teacher	99
2. Check the availability of the required ICT equipment and promptly inform the teacher of any problems with obtaining the equipment needed	99
3. Follow manufacturer's and safety instructions for setting up the ICT equipment	99

Standard 3-17.1: *(continued)*

4.	Make sure that there is ready access to accessories, consumables and information needed to use the equipment effectively	100, 114
5.	Check that the equipment is switched on, ready and safe for use when needed	99
6.	Promptly report any faults with the equipment to both the teacher and the person responsible for arranging maintenance or repair	97, 99, 114
7.	Ensure that any faulty equipment is isolated from any power source, appropriately labelled and made safe and secure.	97, 99, 114
Knowledge base		
You must know and understand:		
a)	The sorts of ICT equipment available within the school and where it is kept	
b)	School procedures for booking or allocating ICT equipment for use in the classroom	
c)	The location and use of accessories, consumables and instructions/information texts	100, 114
d)	Who to report equipment faults and problems to and the procedures for doing this	97, 114

Scope of ICT equipment to which this standard applies

1. Overhead projection equipment

2. Recording and playback equipment

3. Personal computers and peripherals, including printers, modem links, software packages

Standard 3-17.2: Support classroom use of ICT equipment

Performance indicators	
You must show that you:	**Page no.**
1. Operate ICT equipment correctly and safely when asked to do so	99
2. Give clear guidance and instructions on the use of ICT equipment by others	111
3. Give support as needed to help pupils develop skills in the use of ICT	111
4. Provide an appropriate level of assistance to enable pupils to experience a sense of achievement, maintain self-confidence and encourage self-help skills in the use of ICT	
5. Monitor the safe use of equipment by others and intervene promptly where actions may be dangerous	111
6. Regularly check that equipment is working properly and promptly report any faults to the appropriate person	99, 114

Standard 3-17.2: Support classroom use of ICT equipment *(continued)*

7.	Use only approved accessories and consumables	100, 114
8.	Make sure that the equipment is left in a safe condition after use	114
9.	Make sure that the equipment is stored safely and securely after use	
Knowledge base		
You must know and understand:		
a)	Operating requirements and routines	98, 104
b)	Relevant legislation, regulations and guidance in relation to the use of ICT, e.g. copyright, data protection, software licensing, child protection	84, 86 114, 117
c)	The school policy for use of ICT in the classroom including virus controls and access to the Internet	85, 101, 114, 115,
d)	Effective communication of instructions and guidance	108, 111
e)	How to use the software and learning programmes used by the pupils you are working with	23, 111
f)	How to select and use learning packages to match the age and development levels of the pupils with whom you work	23, 111
g)	The range of ICT skills needed by pupils and what can be expected from the age group with which you work	111
h)	How to support the development of ICT skills in pupils	111
i)	How to promote independence in the use of ICT equipment by pupils	111
j)	Risks associated with equipment and how to minimise them	99
k)	Who to report equipment faults and problems to and the procedures for doing this	97, 114
l)	The location and use of accessories and consumables	100, 114
m)	School requirements and procedures for storage and security of ICT equipment	

Scope of ICT equipment to which this standard applies

1. Overhead projection equipment

2. Recording and playback equipment

3. Personal computers and peripherals including printers, modem links and software packages

Scope of skills to which this standard applies

4. Basic user skills

5. Selection and use of appropriate software packages

6. Accessing and using learning programmes

7. Accessing information

8. Using electronic communication systems

Glossary

Here are just a few of the words and abbreviations you will come across when talking about ICT. There are several good glossaries and dictionaries on the Internet and in bookshops if you need to find more.

AAC	Augmentative and alternative technology – additional tools for people with speech and language problems.
absolute cell reference	Part of a spreadsheet formula that does not change when copied to other cells.
application	Software.
assistive technology	Additional tools for people with special needs.
attachment	A document sent with an email that is not part of the message itself.
back up	Make a copy of computer files in case something goes wrong.
bit	Smallest unit that computer files are measured in.
bitmap	Type of graphic file where each point on the screen is logged, like a cross between a graph and painting by numbers.
bookmark	Keep a note of a web page so you can return to it.
Boolean search	Type of search using operators such as '+' or 'AND', '−' or 'NOT' to filter results.
boot	Start up a computer.
broadband	Fast Internet connection.
browser	Software used to access the Internet.
bug	Problem with a computer's software.
byte	Larger unit of measurement for computer files.
CAD/CAM	Computer-aided design/computer-aided manufacture – planning a product on a computer then linking to a machine to create it.

case sensitive	Reacts to upper and lower case letters.
cell	Box on a spreadsheet.
compatability	Ability to link up to other parts of the computer, both hardware and software.
concept keyboard	Flat pad that can control the computer through touch.
cookie	Instructions from a website to a computer that can track use.
CPU	Central processing unit – the bit of the computer that does the working out.
CSV	Comma separated variables – standard format for moving information between databases.
data	Collection of information.
database	Means of managing a collection of information.
dial up	connecting to the Internet over an ordinary telephone line.
digital	Generally something captured in an electronic format such as music or a photo.
domain name	The name and location in a website address.
download	To copy something from one place to another, usually from the Internet.
dpi	Dots per inch – the means of setting the quality of a print-out.
drag and drop	Method of moving text and images around.
FAQ	Frequently asked questions. Usually found on websites.
field	Space each piece of data is entered into.
file	Anything created and saved on a computer.
file extension	The three or four letters after the file's name that tells the computer what program to use to open it.
firewall	Means of preventing hostile attack on a computer from outside.
folder	Place where a collection of files is stored.
font	The type style, the design of the lettering.
formula	A calculation on a spreadsheet.
free text	A field in a database without restrictions on the type or amount of information that can be entered.
FTP	File transfer protocol – a way of getting pages onto the Internet.
GIF	Graphic interchange format – type of image file.
gigabyte	Big unit of measure of computer space.
graphics	Images.
graphics card	Part of the computer that puts the images on screen.
GUI	Graphical user interface – what you see on the screen that you can click on to operate the computer.
hard drive (or disk)	The permanent memory store in the computer, as opposed to a floppy disk which can be removed.

hardware	The machines, wiring and other physical components of a computer that you can touch.
home page	Opening page of a website.
HTML	Hypertext mark-up language – the programming code web pages are written in.
hyperlink	Text or image you can click on that takes you to somewhere else.
icon	Image on screen that represents something, an action or a company for instance.
input device	Means of getting information into the computer, such as a keyboard or microphone.
ISDN	A fast connection to the Internet.
ISP	Internet service provider – a company that connects users to the Internet.
Java	Programming language used on the Internet for games and animations.
JPEG	Type of image file.
LAN	Local area network – group of computers linked together that are in one place.
megabyte	Large unit of measurement for computer files.
MIDI	Hardware that links a computer to a synthesiser.
MLE	Manage Learning Environment – software that sets and marks students work and gives out reports.
modem	Hardware to dial up to the internet.
monitor	The screen.
MPEG	Type of movie file.
multimedia	Bringing text, sound and images together in one creation.
netiquette	Rules of behaviour for Internet users, such as do not use capital letters as it is the equivalent of shouting.
network	Group of computers that are linked together.
newsgroup	Web-based group with a common interest which exchanges information.
notebook	A type of laptop.
OCR	Optical character reader – means of automatically entering information from a written page.
on line	Connected to the Internet.
palmtop	Computer that can be held in the hand.
PC	Computer that uses Microsoft software.
PDA	Personal digital assistant – a sort of palmtop.
PDF	Portable document format – standard format for documents shared on the Internet.
peripheral	Hardware attached to a computer, such as a scanner or printer.

POP 3	A type of email account.
port	Where you link extra devices to the computer.
predictor	Literacy software that suggests the next word the user will want.
program	Software.
QWERTY	Standard keyboard – referring to the top line of letters.
RAM	Random access memory – the working memory on the computer.
ROM	Read only memory – information that cannot be changed.
router	On a network the hardware that decides which route information will take.
RTF	Rich text format – standard format for sharing text files.
search	A way of interrogating information on a database or of finding it on the Internet.
search engine	Web page that helps you find what you are looking for.
search term	The words you use to look things up.
sensor	Device for inputting information such as temperature.
software	The programs and other operating information on a computer, which you cannot touch.
sound card	Part of the computer that handles sound.
speech engine	Software that makes the computer talk.
switch	A means for people with special needs to control a computer.
terrabyte	Biggest unit yet of measuring computer capacity.
touch screen	Screen that controls the computer through a touch-sensitive surface.
tracker ball	Alternative to a mouse where the user rolls the ball directly.
trojan	Type of virus that sneaks up on the computer.
upload	To add files, usually to the Internet.
URL	Uniform resource locator – address of a website.
USB	Universal serial bus – standard way of connecting peripherals.
VDU	Another name for the monitor.
virus	Program that attacks the computer.
VLE	Virtual learning environment – computer-based learning system.
VR	Virtual reality – onscreen depictions of actual or pretend 3D situations.
WAN	Wide area network – computers linked together over a broad geographical area.
wild card	Used in searches to broaden the terms. For instance 'W*' would bring up all entries beginning with 'W'.
wizard	Part of software that helps you to do a job.
worksheet	Working area of a spreadsheet.

write protect	Stop information on a disk from being overwritten.
Wysiwyg	What you see is what you get – when you print something it looks like the screen.
zip	Way of making files smaller to make them easier to move around.

Bibliography and further reading

Ager, Richard (1998) *Information and Communications Technology in Primary Schools.* London: David Fulton Publishers.

Ball, Alison (2004) *Help – There's a computer in my classroom.* London: David Fulton Publishers.

British Computer Society (1997) *IT Glossary for Schools.* Harlow: Longman.

DfES (2002) *Learning Styles and Writing in English.* Department for Education and Science. Crown Copyright.

Ekwall, E. and Shanker, J. (1988) *Diagnosis and Remediation of the Disabled Reader* (3rd Edition). London: Allyn and Bacon.

Gardner, H. (1983) *Frames of Mind: the theory of multiple intelligences.* London: Heinemann.

Local Government National Training Organisation (2001) *National Occupational Standards for Teaching/Classroom Assistants.*

Moran, J., Hull, V. and Wheeler, D. (2003) *The Complete Idiot's Guide to ECDL.* London: Prentice Hall.

Penrose, B. and Pollard, B. (2003) *Complete A–Z ICT and Computing Handbook* (Second edition). London: Hodder and Stoughton.

Sinclair, I. (2003) *Collins Dictionary of Computers and IT.* Glasgow: HarperCollins.

Watkinson, A. (2003) *The Essential Guide for Competent Teaching Assistants.* London: David Fulton Publishers.

There are several series of books about using particular programs. Two of the better ones are the 'For Dummies' series from Wiley Publishing and 'Essential Computers' from Dorling Kindersley. Examples of these are:

Lowe, D. (2001) *Powerpoint 2002 for Dummies.* New York: Wiley Publishing Inc.

Dinwiddie, R. (2002) *Creating Worksheets.* London: Dorling Kindersley.

Index